The Bight of Benin

In the fourteen short stories in this book, the author, Kelly J. Morris, draws upon his fifty-year association with Africa to open a window into the countries bordering the Bight of Benin. A long indentation into the coastline of the Gulf of Guinea, the waters of the Bight of Benin have a strong undertow. It was the source of so many of the enslaved Africans carried off to the Americas that it was called "The Slave Coast." In these stories set in Ghana, Togo, Benin, and Nigeria, we meet the Water Witch, a skinny European brother who claims he can find water with his divining rod; bank employees and African-American immigrants enduring Ghana's hard times; an extension agent demoted to janitor; subsistence farmers struggling in the money economy; civil servants with secure jobs but with enormous family responsibilities; an apprentice truck driver with ambitions for a better life; small business owners trying to make a living and stay in business; women and girls carving out new roles while trying to maintain respect for their culture; devout practitioners of traditional religions, Christianity, and Islam; true believers and charlatans; and many more.

Books by Kelly J. Morris:

Fire in the Tree:
The Inspector Toh-Jay Stories

Second Semester 2020:
Playing the Notes That Aren't There:
Essays, Articles, and Reminiscences
of Africa Since 1968

First Semester 2021:
African Democracy:
A Primer for Development Workers

Second Semester 2021:
Let the Big Cat Jump: Short Stories

The Bight of Benin

Short Fiction by

Kelly J. Morris

SECOND EDITION

COPYRIGHT

Apart from any fair use for the purposes of research, private study, criticism, or review, as permitted under the United States Constitution Article 1, Section 8, Clause 8, known as the Copyright Clause, as implemented by the Copyright Act of 1976, this publication may only be reproduced, stored, or transmitted, in any form or by any means, with the prior permission in writing of the copyright holder. Inquiries concerning reproduction outside those terms should be sent to the copyright holder at: kellyjmorris@gmail.com ..

The use of registered names and trademarks in this book does not imply, even in the absence of a specific statement, that they are exempt from the relevant laws and regulations and therefore free for general use.

This book is a work of fiction. The author makes no representation, express or implied, with regard to the accuracy of the information contained in it and cannot accept any legal responsibility or liability for any errors or omissions that may be made.

Definition: bight

A bend in a coast forming an open bay; as, the Bight of Benin. (*Webster's*)

A long, gradual bend or curve in a shoreline. A bight can be larger than a bay, or it can be a segment of a bay. (*American Heritage*)

The Bight of Benin is located on the western coast of Africa. It begins in Ghana (depending upon which geographer one believes) either at Cape St. Paul, located east of the Volta River at the town of Woe, or at Cape Three Points, south-west of Takoradi. It extends eastward for at least 400 miles (640 km) and ends at the Nun River outlet of the Niger River in Nigeria. It lies within the Gulf of Guinea in the Atlantic Ocean and is bordered by the countries of Ghana, Togo, Benin, and Nigeria. The waters of the Bight of Benin are known for their dangerous undertow. Its long association with the slave trade resulted in the labeling of the area as the "Slave Coast" on early European maps. (*Britannica*)

Watch and beware

O' the Bight o' Benin,

There's few that come out

Tho' many go in!

- Sea Chanty

I first ventured into the Bight of Benin more than fifty years ago and I have never really left.
- Kelly J. Morris

Dedicated

to the

Memory

of

Jennifer Rubin

PREFACE

This second edition of *The Bight of Benin* includes my first short story, *The Water Witch*, that was broadcast on **BBC World Service** radio in 1984 and published in **SELAMTA**, the in-flght magazine of Ethiopean Airlines in 1985, and thirteen additional stories. The stories from the First Edition in which the main character is Inspector Toh-Jay, a crafty, resourceful, and compassionate policeman in a remote district, have been moved--along with several new Toh-jay stories--to a book entitled **Fire in the Tree: The Inspector Toh-jay Stories**. They are replaced in this edition by *AfriChoco*.

These short stories take place in the area of West Africa that is bordered by the Bight of Benin--the countries of Ghana, Togo, Bénin, and Nigeria-- during the period from 1969 to the present. While my career in international development has taken me to most of West and Central Africa, especially the

French-speaking countries, the Bight of Benin countries constitute the core of my experience in Africa.

All of these short stories inevitably have been inspired by people whom I have known, places where I have lived or visited, events that I have witnessed or taken part in, and tales that I have been told. They are true and faithful to these inspirations, but they are not factual. They are fiction

I hope that my stories will open a window into these countries and help others to meet and enjoy their people as I have.

Kelly J. Morris
Maryland USA
December 2020

CONTENTS

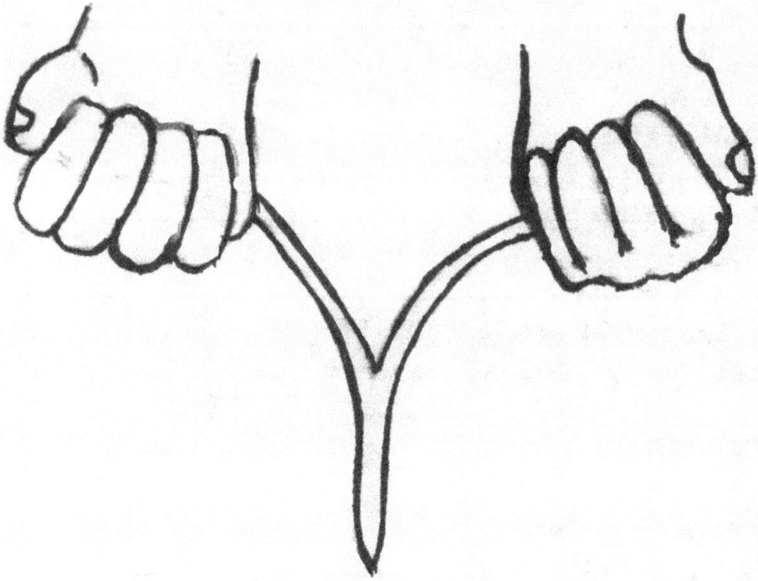

THE WATER WITCH

Santana adjusted the rear-view mirror to get a better look at the Water Witch sitting in the back seat. It was still dark when he and the Community Development Agent arrived to pick him up. Santana had waited in the car while the Agent went inside for coffee with the Water Witch and the other French Brothers. By lamp light, he had his first look at the Water Witch. He was middle-aged, thin with knobby knees showing between his khaki shorts and his khaki socks and sandals. As Santana turned from the dirt road on to the pavement, he could see in the dawn light the Water Witch's balding head and wrinkled brow reflected in the rear-view mirror. Even as he dozed, his eyes squinted with intensity and the veins stood out at his temples.

"He doesn't look like someone who smiles very easily," Santana thought as they sped through a Muslim town at the base of the mountain.

"Are you awake, Brother?" the Community Development Agent asked.

"Oh, yes. I was just dozing a bit. It is going to be a long day and I want to conserve my energy."

"You're quite right to do so, Brother. The people of the village are anxiously awaiting you. They really need water badly, and they're not lazy. But every time we try to get them to dig, they ask, 'How do you know that we'll find water?'"

"Can you really find water, Brother?" Santana interjected.

"Oh, excuse me, Brother," said the Agent. "I didn't properly introduce our driver, Santana. He's also a mechanic and somehow he keeps this old tub running."

"Santana, Santana," said the Water Witch. "Yes. I know the family. You're from the coast, are you? You must be related to Father Santana at the Cathedral."

"Actually, Brother, Santana is not my real name. My brother lives in Accra. A musician named Santana played there for the anniversary of Ghana's independence in 1971. My brother brought me a Santana t-shirt, and from the time I wore it, everyone called me Santana. Most people don't know my real name. It's Braïma, and I'm from this region. I'm a Muslim."

"I don't think I've heard of this Santana fellow, but I don't listen to music, usually. Too much work to do."

"But tell me, Brother," Santana continued, "can you really find water with a forked stick?"

"Yes, of course. I wouldn't waste these poor people's time if I could not. I learned from old Brother Ferdinand. You'll see today."

"I'm looking forward to it," said Santana as he crested the mountain and began to weave down the other side. Across the way, a roof came into view among the treetops.

"Speaking of Brother Ferdinand, there's the monastery," exclaimed the Community Development Agent. "Even though I spent more than six years there, I never bothered to learn how to find water."

"Oh, you went to seminary?" asked the Water Witch.

"Yes, Brother. And I got quite a good education. But when it came time to decide about ordination, I decided that being a priest wasn't right for me."

"It seems that many young men get a good education there and then come to the same decision," said the Water Witch with more than a hint of sarcasm.

"I like to think that I'm serving God in what I do now, Brother--trying to help the people of these poor villages to improve their lives," said the Agent as he turned around in his seat.

"Certainly," said the Water Witch.

They continued south to the regional capital in silence, passing through the foothills with a small village every seven or eight kilometers. Santana braked to a halt at the Gendarmerie. It was seven o'clock, and they all stood in silence as the Gendarmes raised the flag. As they drove across town, the streets were awash with the khaki uniforms of children hurrying off to school. By the time they reached the other side of town, the children were already in lines in front of their classrooms, ready to enter. When they turned east, Santana flipped down the visor and put on his dark glasses.

"It's about ninety kilometers to the village, Brother," said the Agent. "The road hasn't been scraped in some time. We'll just count on our friend Santana to avoid the worst of the potholes."

Santana leaned forward in his seat and held the steering wheel firmly in both hands. He maneuvered deftly around holes, accelerated briskly to skip over the washboard, and managed to miss the many people, chickens, and goats in the road as he sped through the villages in the low, rolling hills. It was the dry season and brown and yellow were the colors of everything, except for the occasional green of trees with deep roots that dotted the grassland.

As they sped through a small village, they passed a large white mound, with a dozen women sitting around it with pieces of multicolored cloth.

"What's that?" asked the Water Witch.

"Kapok, Brother," said Santana. "The women are making pillows."

"Sitting on their buttocks making pillows to sit better on their buttocks!" said the Water Witch, his voice dripping with venom. His comment was so unexpected and so bitter that the Agent turned around in his seat and stared at him open-mouthed, before turning silently back and staring at the road ahead.

When they rolled into the village, they found it alive and busy with market-day activities. School had just come-out for mid-morning recess. The children deserted the women selling bananas and groundnuts and porridge to run alongside the Land Rover, squealing with delight as the vehicle made its way across the schoolyard to the mango tree. There, the school Principal and teachers, the village Chief, several elders and a number of women were waiting.

"You're right on time," said the Principal to the Community Development Agent.

"And so are you," replied the Agent.

"Oh, I'm no fool, my friend. I asked them to come at seven. They have just arrived." The two shared a laugh as they walked toward the group.

After a round of greetings, introductions, and handshakes, the Agent and the Water Witch sat down in the straight-back chairs provided for them. The

Principal's children brought cool water in porcelain-covered metal mugs. The Principal immediately put his case to the Water Witch, explaining in great detail the necessity for a new well.

"Since the well caved in, we've really been suffering. The children have no water to drink, and we have to pay to have water for our families carried from the stream. And dirty water at that."

"Let's see this well," said the Water Witch as he sprung to his feet. He reached inside his sack and drew out a smooth forked stick. Each of the three parts was about 30 centimeters long. He tested it quickly--holding the forks and watching the other end bobbing up and down as if tied to an invisible string.

"Follow me," said the Principal.

They descended a gentle slope in between two classroom buildings.

The well was in a shallow area surrounded by mango trees beyond the open end of the schoolyard. Across the way was the market place from which the people eyed the Water Witch with curiosity.

"Did this well ever dry up in the dry season?" asked the Water Witch.

"No, Brother. Never."

"How far down was the water?"

"See for yourself, Brother."

They all walked to the well and peered over the edge. After their eyes adjusted from the sunlight to the dark, they could see that the bricks that lined the well had caved-in at the bottom. But through the jumble of bricks they could see the water.

"How far down to the water?"

"About nine meters, Brother."

"All right. Let's see if we can find a place for a new well."

The Water Witch surveyed the crowd that had gathered for the market. All the village was there, it seemed--farmers in from their fields, the goat sellers from up north, the women from the northwest who crossed the mountain to trade homemade soap for porcelain pans and grain, and small groups of people gossiping around the pots of millet beer. The trading and gossiping of the market had been rarely interrupted by spectacle. Once, "The Strongest Man in the World" pulled a market lorry with a rope. Another time, two turbaned Touaregs came through on camels, and charged ten francs to make the camels kneel. The crowd waited with curiosity to see what this thin little Frenchman with a forked stick had to offer. They were not disappointed.

The Water Witch grasped a branch of the forked stick firmly in each hand, knitted his brow in concentration, and then started walking. Wandering, it seemed at first, with a crowd of noisy children following along. Then suddenly the Water Witch would tear off in one direction or another, as if dragged by an invisible force tugging at his witching stick. His forays led him back and forth, into the high grass on one side, emerging in full stride at another point, sweating profusely and plunging directly into the family compounds on the other side. Then he shot off across the market as if drawn by a team of runaway horses. People staggered away from their millet beer to stare at him. The children were delighted and streamed after him. As his path brought him by the Land Rover, he stopped and cried out in exasperation.

"This takes so much concentration. Can't you get them to stop?"

While the Water Witch caught his breath, Santana spoke.

"You know, Brother, when I see you pulled here and there by your stick, you remind me of the people up north."

"How is that?" snapped the Water Witch with obvious irritation.

"Well, when someone dies there, the family carries the body around the village. And sometimes, they seem to be pulled off in one direction or another. They say it's the dead person making them take him to visit the tree he rested under, or the field he farmed, or his mother's family house before they put him in the ground."

"That's just a bunch of ignorant superstition," huffed the Water Witch, "and it does not have anything to do with what I do."

He returned to his task.

The Water Witch's wanderings eventually became more and more concentrated at a single spot and the crowd closed in around him. Finally, he stopped in his tracks, knitted his brow, and tensed his grip in concentration. He rotated slowly and the point of the stick would dip toward the ground when it passed over the spot and rise to level again each time it passed away from it.

"Here," he cried.

Everyone rushed to surround him.

"Dig here. You're sure to find water."

"How deep, Brother?"

"Just a minute," replied the Water Witch.

Santana had elbowed his way to front of the crowd. He looked at the spot that the Water Witch had chosen and then he looked over his shoulder at the old well. They were not ten meters apart. When he looked back, the Water Witch had taken a motorcycle spark plug out of his pocket. At its tip, it was tied to a string. The Water Witch dangled the spark from his left hand. With his right hand, he set the spark plug swinging clockwise and began counting each full swing.

"One, two, three. . ."

The spark plug slowed down with each rotation. When the Water Witch reached nine, he quickly snapped the plug back into his hand.

"Nine," he said. "Nine meters. If you dig here you'll hit water at nine meters."

The Water Witch triumphantly received the acclaim of the crowd. The Chief and the Community Development Agent made their way to him and pumped his hand in congratulation. Santana had followed them and the Water Witch spotted him.

"Well now, Mr. Santana, are you convinced now that I can find water?"

"Not at all, Brother. With the old well right here with water in it, it would seem to be hard to fail."

"All right," cried the Water Witch angrily. "Try it and you'll see." He shoved the witching stick into Santana's hands and guided him to the spot where he had been standing.

Santana grasped the forked stick firmly in his hands and the crowd became silent. Imitating the Water Witch, he rotated slowly, bringing the point of the stick across the spot. But nothing happened. When he rotated back across the spot again with the same result, the crowd gasped and the Water Witch came running over.

"No, no, no," he said. "You're doing it all wrong. I'll show you."

He swiftly moved beside Santana. Santana held a fork in each hand and the Water Witch grasped him firmly by the wrists. As they rotated toward the spot, the Water Witch slowly, imperceptibly but firmly pulled Santana's hands away from each other, causing the point to bend toward the ground at the spot. As they completed the rotation away from the spot, the Water Witch just as artfully pulled Santana's hands back toward each other, causing the point to rise back to level.

A cheer went up from the crowd as the Water Witch snatched the witching stick from Santana and strode away with the Chief and the Agent.

"We'll begin digging tomorrow," the Chief promised.

Santana was waiting for them in the Land Rover. He said nothing as they got in and sped off into the sunset. He could see the Water Witch in the rear-view mirror. Red-faced, exhausted, and sweaty, he had refused food and drink all day. And now he winced with great irritation at every bump in the road, as if each one were an insult directed at his person.

"I think our driver is tired," said the Water Witch archly.

Santana smiled to himself, pressed firmly on the accelerator pedal, and aimed the Land Rover squarely at the biggest pothole he could see.

THE FULANI COW

It was the middle of the night when Nkrumah raised himself from his mat, gathered his goatskin bag, and slipped silently out of his house. He looked carefully around as he stole out of his compound and down the path. The moon was full. He might meet a group of revelers who took advantage of the cool of the night and the bright moonlight to sing and dance and gossip or women getting an early start carrying water to be finished in time for market day. As it turned out, he had chosen his moment well and met no one. The stubble of the millet stalks was all that remained in the fields, so he moved quickly from shadow to shadow until he reached the path leading out of the village.

Halfway to the ridge west of the village, Jerry was waiting for him where the paths from their villages joined. Jerry was a cousin whose people had left many years ago after a quarrel to found their own village a few kilometers away. Nkrumah and Jerry had always gotten on well, though, ever since the time when they lived near each other in the Nima quarter of Accra, the capital of Ghana.

"Fine morning, sah!" Nkrumah relished the chance to use the little English he remembered.

Jerry responded with an irritated grimace to his cousin's indiscreetly hearty greeting and motioned silently for him to follow.

"Where are your butcher's tools?" exclaimed Nkrumah. His cousin was carrying only a couple of ropes.

"I hid them at our spot," hissed Jerry. "We're going to have our hands full as it is. Keep quiet!"

They crested the ridge and looked down to a wide flat valley bottom. The Fulani compounds on the valley floor stood out in the moonlight. They left the path and moved down the ridge to a shelf of rock surrounded by trees and bushes.

"We'll be safe here," said Jerry.

They could see the valley clearly while lying on the flat rock, yet in daylight they would be out of sight. Jerry quickly fell asleep. He was much less gregarious since the Accra days, when his love of music had won him the name Jerry Hanson, after the great Ghanaian highlife musician. But then, he had little to be happy about since the Ghanaians took away everything he had.

Before December 1969, Jerry had joined some Hausa butchers and learned their trade. He had converted to Islam like his Hausa friends and underwent the painful required circumcision. He adopted a Muslim name, dressed in a long *boubou* and round cap like his friends, and came to speak their language perfectly. The butchers trusted him as a fellow Muslim and provided him with loans and expert advice needed to start his own business. He made a little money, opened a kiosk in Nima, and finally bought a building lot in the suburb of Madina.

All that ended quickly when he was gathered up with his Hausa friends, put in a truck, and sped to the border with tens of thousands of other foreigners who were expelled from Ghana. The police were ready to wave the truck straight through Togo on its way to Nigeria when he convinced them that there was someone inside who wanted out. Get out he did, with only the shirt on his back. He was then transported to Northern Togo where he arrived penniless in his thoroughly non-Muslim place of birth. Since then, he occupied himself exclusively with farming. He prayed irregularly at home and rarely presented himself in town at the mosque across from the market.

Nkrumah could not blame Jerry for his lack of humor. He, too, had nothing to show for his years in Ghana but he did not take it quite so hard. Perhaps it was because he never had much to lose. When he tired of digging graves in Accra's cemeteries, he came back to the village with nothing but a battery-powered phonograph and quickly acquired the nickname "Nkrumah."

Unable to sleep, he lay on his belly and looked out over the valley. It was silent except for the occasional stirring of a cow in the enclosures by the Fulanis' compounds.

"Their houses look just like ours," he thought, "except that beneath the conical straw roof are not mud walls but woven mats. Jerry said that makes it easier for them to break camp at night and steal off with the cattle people entrusted to them. The Fulanis on the other side of the mountain had done just that a couple of years ago with eighty head. 'Stealing a cow from a Fulani,' Jerry said, 'would be like taking back something already stolen.' All the same, these Fulanis seem all right."

"They train their cows." Jerry's voice startled Nkrumah out of his thoughts. "I was out here on market day a few weeks ago. They leave the cattle with no one to watch them when they go to market. But you never know what to expect. The Hausas told me about one who had his herd trained to protect him. They would surround him with their horns pointed outward whenever there was danger."

Dawn was creeping up behind them and there was activity in the compounds. It was more than two hours before Boukari and his family set out toward the market. Nkrumah could make out Boukari in his wide-brimmed, pointed hat striding out in front with his staff across his shoulders. Jerry insisted on waiting until they were out of sight before they began their descent.

The cattle were outside their enclosures, grazing intently, trying to find some hint of moisture in the brown and yellow grass. Some were ambling toward the small ponds of water in the stream-bed. The two men slowly made their way and Jerry spoke in hushed tones.

"What we must do," he said when they were about fifty meters from the cattle, "is to pick out one and go for it. We must not run about chasing after one and then another."

"I see one!" cried Nkrumah as he burst off to chase the nearest animal.

"Wait, you fool," yelled Jerry angrily, but it was too late. Having followed Jerry's lead up to this point, something possessed Nkrumah to take the initiative. Jerry could do nothing but join in the chase.

The moment that Nkrumah began his charge, the seemingly listless, passive beasts began fleeing toward the ends of the valley. Jerry arrived just in time to save Nkrumah from being impaled on the horns of his animal. He quickly slipped the noose of the rope onto a hind leg and brought the animal down by tying the two hind legs together. Jerry sat on its rump and caught his breath.

The rest of the cattle were gone. He looked down and shouted.

"It's a cow!"

"What difference does it make?" asked Nkrumah.

Jerry did not respond. At this point, it made no difference. He moved up and tied the second rope around the cow's horns.

Jerry handed the horn rope to Nkrumah and untied one hind leg. The cow sprang to its feet and lunged toward Nkrumah, only to be stopped by Jerry's firm hold on the leg rope. Nkrumah pulled in his direction and they went off, the cow stretched between them.

It took them three hours to push and pull the cow over the hill to the path leading from the market. When the cow's head rope was secured to a shady mango tree by the side of the path and the leg rope tied to a nearby tree, Jerry retrieved his butcher's tools from under a bush.

He dispatched the cow quickly and began butchering it. People would soon be returning from the market and they needed to be ready to sell meat.

"She had a calf!" yelled Jerry as Nkrumah returned with a bunch of leaves for wrapping.

Nkrumah shrugged his shoulders and returned to his work. By the time Jerry finished, the first people came down the path and a brisk business began. With meat selling at half-price, few people could resist parting with some of their money from the sale of grain or clay pots. Word spread back into the village and Nkrumah's neighbors were soon among their customers. By dusk, they had sold all the meat. Jerry took the hide and rolled it up to dry in the sun the following day. They counted the money and it came to a little more than sixteen thousand francs. Nkrumah put the money into his bag, thanked his cousin, and they separated in the night.

The police arrested them the next morning. Jerry was in his farm building a rain shelter. Nkrumah was standing in a line at the hospital pharmacy. They met in the district jail, a stone building with a tin roof and no windows--only a few airholes at the top of the walls. When they tried to ask a question, the policeman replied, "tomorrow," and left them alone.

"How did they find out?" Nkrumah asked in the darkness.

"There is no lack of people who are ready to betray you," Jerry replied. "We will see what happens tomorrow." He stretched out on a thin mat and was soon asleep.

At dawn the next day their families brought them water and bean cakes with pepper sauce. At nine o'clock, a policeman with an ancient rifle slung over his shoulder led them to a bench outside the office of the Judge where they sat down across from Boukari the Fulani, his brother, and their sons. The Fulanis whispered knowingly in their language and then were quiet.

The Judge was a stocky man with salt-and-pepper hair and a long, bearded chin. The local people called him "Ojukwu" after the Biafaran secessionist leader that he so closely resembled. He called the two cousins into his office where he was seated behind his desk. The court clerk stood to his right. The Fulanis sat across from the Judge, while Nkrumah and Jerry stood with the policeman.

"All right, Mr. Clerk," said the Judge, "tell me about this cow."

The clerk explained that Boukari, upon returning from the market, found his cattle returning from the ends of the valley. In the moonlight, he tracked the missing cow to the place where it was butchered. Boukari then went to the police, who had no trouble finding people in Nkrumah's village who admitted buying meat from the two cousins at their shade-tree butcher shop.

The Judge asked Boukari a few questions and ascertained that the cow was carrying a calf and that he, not someone from the village, was the owner.

"What do you have to say for yourselves?" said the Judge, turning to Nkrumah and Jerry. Jerry started to speak but Nkrumah, displaying the same unexpected initiative that he had shown in chasing the cow, beat him to the start.

"I don't see why we're here," he said indignantly. "Everyone knows Fulanis are nothing but thieves. They're always running off with other people's cattle. Taking a cow from them is just taking back something already stolen."

Jerry grimaced at hearing his words parroted back, and turned his face to the wall.

"If you have a complaint," said the Judge, "then make it to the police. But until then, we're talking about you and your partner stealing a cow." Turning to the clerk, he asked, "How much was the cow worth?"

"Thirty thousand," replied the clerk after conferring with Boukari.

The Judge turned to Nkrumah. "The penalty for stealing a cow is twice the price--that's sixty thousand. A cow with calf counts as two cows, so that's one hundred twenty thousand francs you owe these Fulanis!"

Nkrumah sank to his knees, trembling.

"That's in addition to any time you spend in prison," added the Judge.

Nkrumah groaned just as there was a knock at the door. The policeman opened the door and a thin, neatly dressed man in his late thirties entered. It was Master Baouba, the Principal of the Mission School in Nkrumah's village.

"Good morning, Master," said the Judge. "What can I do for you?"

"Good morning, Judge," replied Baouba. "May I speak to you about he case before you? I have some information that I hope will be of interest."

"Take them outside," the Judge ordered. Nkrumah and Jerry again found themselves in the hall facing the Fulanis.

"Now, Master Baouba," continued the Judge, "what have you to tell us?"

"I thought you should know why Nkrumah and Jerry stole the cow," said Baouba.

"Why, to get money of course," said the Judge with a smile.

"Yes, that's true, but not everyone steals to get money," said Baouba. He launched into an account of the pair's years in Accra and the disappointment with which they had returned empty-handed to their villages.

"Master, there are many people from this district who went to Accra to find work and many who are still there," said the Judge, "but they didn't turn to stealing."

"That's quite true," said Baouba, "but I think that this is the reason for the theft." He handed a slip of paper to the Judge.

"A pharmacy prescription with prices totaling fifteen thousand eight hundred forty-seven francs. How is this the cause?" asked the Judge.

"It's for Nkrumah's wife. She has been quite sick for several weeks. Nkrumah took her to some of our local healers. They have many herbs that are effective but they were not able to help her. When they finally took her to the hospital, they found out what it was but the prescriptions were expensive. By this time, Nkrumah had spent all of his money and it was the second half of the month so no one had any money left to lend him. He turned to his cousin Jerry for help and they cooked up this scheme. They were desperate."

"Call the doctor," ordered the Judge.

"He's not back yet," said the Clerk. "He's still in the capital."

"Then call in the Head Nurse."

The Clerk went out and came back a half hour later with an earnest-looking man in a white frock coat. Nkrumah, Jerry, and the Fulanis returned to the Judge's office.

"Did you write this prescription?" the Judge asked as he passed the slip of paper across the desk.

"Yes, Judge. It's for Nkrumah's wife."

"I know. What are all these things on the list?"

"The first one's an anti-biotic. Then there are some fortifiers--vitamins, that is. Something to stimulate her appetite. Something to help her sleep. And, of course, something for her liver."

"Do you mean that these two fools were led to steal for some vitamins and liver pills?" the Judge said as he leaned across the table.

The Head Nurse looked bewildered.

"The doctor isn't here," he explained, "so I did the best I could--what I thought he would do. It's an infectious disease, so I prescribed an anti-biotic. She's weak so she needs to get her strength back with vitamins and a good appetite and sleep."

"What's the matter with her liver?"

"Everyone knows how important the liver is . . ."

"Did it ever occur to you to get fruit from the market instead of vitamin injections? And don't you have some herbs to brew up to help her sleep and eat better?"

The Head Nurse said nothing.

"And she's not a Frenchman to be taking liver pills all the time! You can go now."

"I'd have told him to get the anti-biotic and not bother with the rest if he had only told me his problem," said the Head Nurse before going out the door.

The Judge drummed his desktop with his fingers and stared out the window, as if hoping he would find a Solomonic solution out there.

Master Baouba broke the silence.

"Judge, I have a cow. Boukari is keeping her for me. And she's carrying a calf."

"And how will these two pay you?"

"We'll take care of that in the family, the way we should have in the first place."

"And his wife?"

"We've already bought the anti-biotic and they've given her the injections."

"You're lucky to have such good friends," said the Judge, turning to Nkrumah and Jerry. "But don't let me see you in here again, or there'll be no mercy!" The Judge's stern admonition could not hide his relief.

"You saved us from jail," said Jerry to Baouba when they were outside, "not to speak of one hundred twenty thousand."

"How will we ever repay you?" asked Nkrumah. "I still don't know what to do."

"We failed you," replied Master Baouba solemnly. "If we had helped you when you needed it, you wouldn't have gotten into this mess. Together we will find a solution."

MAÏMOUNA

"Oh, Father, I feel so superior to my fellow teachers!"

The Polish priest was stunned. The other young Americans who had taught English at the secondary school on the Mission grounds had never expressed such a thought. He took advantage of the requirements of African hospitality to buy time for a response.

"I'm going to have a beer. Would you like one?" he said as he moved to the kerosene-powered refrigerator.

"Just water, Father."

Returning to the couch, Father Voytek studied his guest as he poured. Young Michael O'Hara was neat and never seemed to sweat. He never missed mass and always sat in the front row. As a teacher, he was well-respected, punctual, and conscientious.

"Father."

"Just call me Voytek."

"Father, I feel so superior to them."

"My son," Voytek began. He cringed at the words, liking them no more than "Father," but they were appropriate to the occasion.

"It's been a generation at most that our African brothers and sisters have had the benefits that the Mission brought--the education, the clinic, and, of course, the Church--and yet they've made great strides. Just because we've had the advantages of growing up in Europe or America doesn't mean that we're ..."

"Oh, Father, you've missed the point entirely," Michael interrupted. "I didn't mean superior in that way!"

Voytek was both relieved and confused.

"In what way did you mean it?"

"Morally."

"Morally?"

"It's the girls."

Voytek was beginning to understand. Michael took great interest in his students. He was always available to explain, to answer questions, and to tutor, but he was scrupulously correct. Only male students were allowed to come to his house. Female students were helped on school grounds and only before dark. Michael's colleagues, on the other hand, were more than happy to invite schoolgirls to their homes.

"You know what they're doing. That's all they talk about on Monday morning--the schoolgirls they've had during the weekend."

"There's not much we can do about the teachers' behavior," Voytek replied. "The school and the clinic are still on the grounds of the Mission but now the State runs them, and not badly either."

"You have to remember," he continued, "that many of these girls are not so young. They start school late. Many stay back more than once because they're learning in a language that is not their own. By the time they get to secondary school, they're young women, and quite seductive ones at that."

"That's the same excuse the they're always using," Michael exclaimed. "Surely you can't accept that."

"Of course not," Voytek replied. "All I'm saying is that your fellow teachers are human and weak. You should try to reason with them and not be so judgmental."

"I'm not weak like that," said Michael as he headed for the door. "And I hope you're not either."

Voytek watched him stride out of the yard and down the dusty street toward his house. Michael was referring to Voytek's predecessors, Father Marcel, whose three children by different mothers were his students, and Father Michel, who toured remote village markets on his gray Vespa scooter, adding to his photo collection of bare-breasted maidens.

"No, I'm not weak like that," Voytek thought. "In other ways, but not like that."

On Monday, the teachers gathered outside at mid-morning. They exchanged complaints of particularly recalcitrant students and inevitably gossiped about the weekend's pleasures. They snacked on fried yam chips and pepper sauce, and drank gourds of the thick brown sorghum beer that village women sold from their clay pots.

A girl in her khaki skirt and white blouse approached the group and, after a shy curtsy, returned a book to a smart young teacher. He dismissed her with a lingering handshake. After she left, he broke into a lascivious grin and gleefully snapped his fingers together.

"No, you're joking," exclaimed another teacher jealously. "I didn't know she was 'working' already.'"

"Oh, I'm not the first," he replied.

The group commented admiringly on the girl's beauty and physical attributes, after which he regaled them with graphic descriptions of her delights.

"You are disgusting," Michael spat as he stormed back inside.

Seïdou followed him.

"Why are you so upset, Michael? What they're doing is only natural. Besides," he laughed mischievously, "half of what they say is a lie."

"Seïdou, I don't understand you," said Michael. "You've lived in Europe and been to university. You should know how wrong it is."

"Is that what I was supposed to learn in Europe--not to sleep with secondary school girls?" Seïdou replied. "On the contrary, the Frenchmen that I knew thought it was quite a coup for a man to have a teenage mistress. Don't tell me Americans don't do the same."

"We most certainly do not," retorted Michael angrily.

The bell sounded. Seïdou looked at Michael, who was standing rigid, his fists clenched at his side, staring at the table.

"Michael, in spite of what you think, our colleagues are concerned with the students' welfare and try to do a good job."

"I know," said Michael, "but it's still not right."

Mondays were terrible days for Michael--four class periods before noon, and each one a different grade. By fourth period he was tired and the midday sun was beating down on the corrugated tin roof. And fourth period meant Maïmouna with the hypnotic eyes.

Maïmouna's deep black skin set off her enormous, flashing white eyes.

Her features were different--not European, but almost Asian. Her ethnic group was a mixture of the local people and other groups from all over West Africa who had come to a commercial crossroads town. The result was a mini-melting pot of handsome people. Among them, Maïmouna was an outstanding beauty. Her strict Muslim parents had kept her untouched.

As hot and tired as he was in fourth period, it was all Michael could do to keep his mind on his work and his eyes off of Maïmouna. Once he found himself staring at her, only to be brought to his senses by the ripple of giggles that began with Maïmouna and swept across the room. After class, he watched her as she fled the school grounds. Among the shorter and rounder girls, she stood out tall and thin, moving in a graceful, elegant glide compared to her peers' loose-jointed adolescent ambling. Later, she came to the teachers' room for tutoring. Michael relentlessly elicited questions from her that he answered at great length, gazing deep into her eyes for signs of comprehension.

The next day, Michael walked into the faculty room to find a letter waiting for him in his box. He ripped it open eagerly.

Dear Mr. O'Hara,

I take up my pen to write you this little note, and also to inquire about your health. As for me, I am fine and wish you good health and long life.

Only, Dear Mr. O'Hara, I can no longer sleep at night for thinking of you. I was thrilled to learn that I was to study English with an American. Ever since the beginning of the school year, I can't keep you out of my mind. Oh, Mr. O'Hara, please don't be vexed with me. Do you notice me looking at you? I try not to stare, but sometimes I can't help myself.

Am I foolish to hope that you think of me, too? We must talk alone. Shall we try the last day of exams--Friday of next week? We can meet in the evening. I'll steal away at ten o'clock and meet you in the study hall. It's the one with the electric lights.

I won't sleep till then. Please, Mr. O'Hara, accept the respects of

your adorable little Maïmouna

Michael's hand trembled till the paper rattled. He felt hot. He closed his eyes but his head began to spin. He grabbed the edge of the table to keep from falling.

"Are you all right, Michael?" asked Seïdou.

"I'm fine. It's just the heat," Michael replied as he blinked his eyes open.

"Is it bad news?" Seïdou inquired sympathetically with a nod to the letter.

"What? Oh, no. It's a letter from a student's parents asking me to be tough on him if he doesn't work hard." He hurried off to his next class.

Exam period was hectic. Michael was fortunate that teachers proctor and correct the exams of each other's classes. He carefully avoided more than a glimpse of Maïmouna the entire time. He corrected exams and, as his own students' scores came back, recorded them and calculated the term grade.

Friday finally arrived.

It was a perfect night for a rendezvous. The sky was clear, but the moon wouldn't rise until later. Fortified with cologne, Michael went down the road to the school grounds just before ten. He walked silently by the sleeping night watchman and moved toward the classroom that served as a study hall. The campus was dark. The only lights were at Father Voytek's house behind the church. Michael's stomach knotted in anticipation. Fantasy images of himself with Maïmouna flashed across his mind with dizzying speed. He stumbled on the steps and felt his way to the door. As he turned the door knob, he heard a stirring in the room. He opened the door slowly and heard noises closer to him as he entered.

"Maïmouna. Maïmouna!" he called out in a loud whisper.

Just then, he was blinded by lights as they lit up the room. He staggered and looked around to see the laughing faces of all of his fellow teachers.

"Mr. O'Hara! Mr. O'Hara!" they cried in girlish falsetto.

Doubling up with laughter, Seïdou approached him.

Michael stammered, "I was looking for my notebook . . ."

"Then why did you tip-toe in here whispering 'Maïmouna?'" cried Seïdou.

Seïdou regained his composure and clamped an elder-brotherly hand on Michael's shoulder. Michael stared ashamedly at the floor.

"Maïmouna didn't write you, Michael. I did," Seïdou said.

Michael continued to look down.

"I just wanted to show you that we black people aren't as stupid as you think we are!"

"I know you're not, Seïdou. I'm so ashamed of myself."

"Don't take it so hard, boy. We're still your friends. Here, have a beer."

A tall green bottle of beer was shoved into Michael's hands and he brought it to his lips and downed a quarter of it. The cold liquid brought a sweat to his skin. "Why is there beer in the study hall?" he wondered. Benches and desks were being pushed to the walls, cases of drinks appeared, and Congolese music blared from a tape recorder. Some girls came through the door and were quickly dragged onto the dance floor. The sound of shuffling feet joined the music and animated conversation.

Michael was confused and sank into the chair that Seïdou brought him. He took another long draught of beer. Seïdou sat down beside him.

"It's been a long, hot tiring term, hasn't it, Michael? Well, we decided that if we were going to get together to teach you a little lesson, we might as well make a party of it. So, enjoy, Michael. Relax."

Michael managed a weak smile and continued to attack his beer. He finished it quickly. His colleague Yao replaced it and sat down to talk. Beer followed beer and Michael's tongue loosened enough for him to join in one lively discussion after another about sports, politics, weather, teaching. Conversation is African television, the teachers said.

The beer ran out after midnight and the group dispersed, the discussion to continue later. Michael was unsteady on his feet and accepted a lift from a colleague with a scooter. He got off at the side of the road and wobbled down the path to his house.

As he fumbled with his key at the door, he heard noises in the open-air shower stall to the right.

"Mr. O'Hara," a voice called out.

"Huh? Who is it?" Michael responded dumbly.

"It's me, Maïmouna . . ."

TURKEYS

"How does he do that?" asked Yao.

"How does who do what?" responded Kojo with a smile. He already knew who, at least, but he liked to tease his cousin for starting conversations in the middle.

"Long Neck. I hadn't really finished explaining my project to him, when he got up and started walking to the door, talking all the way. Then, he reached out to shake my hand and the next thing I knew, I was out in the reception area, standing there like a fool."

"Well, being the American ambassador's cook in one of Africa's most important port cities does make me privy to certain secrets ..."

"Secrets? You mean like ..."

"No, not that kind. But I can tell you how he did it. They call it the 'diplomatic handshake.' One night, after all the guests had left a reception at

Long Neck's residence, the Americans stayed behind. There was a young couple there--this is their first post--and all the others showed them how to do it. To keep people moving down a receiving line, you reach out to shake the person's hand with both of yours. But instead of moving up and down, you move down and sideways in one swoop with all the weight of your body behind you. The guest then finds himself in front of the next person in the receiving line. It's quite clever, don't you think?"

Yao scowled and did not respond.

"I thought that the American government said it wanted to help Africans?" he asked after a while, and this time Kojo did not respond. "After all, I'm a private businessman. And I produce food!"

"Let's get something to eat," said Kojo. They left the bright lights that lit up the outside walls of Long Neck's white palace where Yao had waited for Kojo to get off work and walked toward the center of town.

When Yao had asked him to ask Long Neck for an appointment, it took Kojo a while to get up the courage.

"Yes, of course," had been Long Neck's reply. "I pride myself in the fact that I never refuse to see anyone, great or small." Kojo didn't know how to take that comment, but he decided to be pleased that Long Neck held him in such high esteem as to grant him a favor without hesitation.

They walked out of the elite residential area and down the deserted main boulevard past locked shops and offices. A large knot of young men crowded around the window of a television and stereo store. Through the wire mesh barrier that covered the window, they watched two color televisions. One was tuned to the local station that showed the parades and speeches and synchronized dancing and slogan-chanting for the state visit of another African president to their own. The other showed a karate movie on videocassette and elicited a much more animated reaction.

"He kept on talking about technical assistance, and how the American government can't finance individuals, only groups. I tried to tell him that I don't need technical assistance. I know how to raise birds--I have a poultry farm. If it's going to be successful, I've got to expand. I don't need advice, I need money! I need to buy feed and vaccines and day-old chicks. I need to build more coops and an incubator. I can't have a modern poultry farm if no one will lend me any money."

They reached the crossroads where women were selling foods that they cooked on charcoal grills. Yao and Kojo sat down on wooden benches and waited patiently for the yam chips and turkey tails to finish cooking. They attacked them when they were hot from the oil and dipped them into pepper sauce as they ate.

Kojo stopped to let his mouth cool off and to wipe the sweat from his forehead.

"When I told Madame Long Neck how much we liked turkey tails from America, she laughed. She said that most Americans don't even know that turkeys have tails--they're cut off before they wrap them in plastic and send them to the supermarket. She was surprised that they sold them to us--she thought that they fed them to pigs or threw them away."

"Threw them away?" Yao was indignant at the thought of such waste.

"She said that it was really ironic that we are eating the tails of American turkeys, while the Americans here are waiting for turkeys for the big feast, and they are stuck in a ship down the coast at Lagos harbor."

Yao almost choked on his food.

"What? They're bringing in turkeys from America? Why don't they just buy them from me?"

"Don't think I didn't suggest that already. But she insists that the turkeys have to come from America. It's for their harvest feast--they call it Thanksgiving."

"Long Neck and the others are not farmers."

"It's a custom. The Americans from all over the country will come for it-- the technical assistants, the missionaries, the Peace Corps Volunteers, the people from the mine--but the turkey feast won't have any turkey."

"Oh, yes it will," said Yao as he stood up to pay the woman. "Sister, who sells you your turkey tails?"

She gave him the name of a well-known local businessman, one of the wealthiest men in town.

"Let's go see him."

"Now? It's almost midnight."

"He's a businessman like me. Businessmen don't sleep."

Kojo accompanied Yao to the man's house, but was too embarrassed to go in. He waited outside. He could see the doors of the freezer lockers inside the compound and hear the noise of the diesel generator. The night watchman dozed against a refrigerated container from the port. A few minutes later, Yao returned at a brisk walk.

"I know who to see now," he said. Kojo could see Yao's brain scheming overtime and felt a twinge of apprehension.

"I'm lucky to have a job," he thought, "and a reasonably good-paying one at that. I hope Yao doesn't do something that will put me out on the street like those jobless boys watching the televisions."

Yao didn't return to his farm that night. He stretched out on a thin mat on the concrete floor at Kojo's rooms in a long, low tin-roofed building made up of a string of two-room apartments. Kojo left for Long Neck's at 6:00 a.m.

but Yao had already left to visit Enyonam the market lady. When one has a service to ask, it's best to go first thing in the morning, he had reminded Kojo.

Kojo was distracted all day as he tried to fend off images of what Yao might be up to and what trouble he might cause him. At lunch, Long Neck had stepped on the button hidden under the carpet beneath the dining room table but Kojo was so lost in his thoughts that he didn't hear the buzzer summoning him. When he didn't pad noiselessly out to the table with the next course, Long Neck actually left his guests and came back to the kitchen to call him. Long Neck was not amused, and there would be no more favors anytime soon.

Yao was waiting for Kojo that night as the guard let him out of the gate of Long Neck's compound.

"I've got good news," said Yao.

"My news isn't so good," replied Kojo. "Madame Long Neck says that they are going to cancel the feast because the ship is going to be delayed for several more weeks."

"Cancel it? They can't do that! Listen, tomorrow morning, tell Madame Long Neck that I can bring her all the American turkeys she needs. I'll wait outside so that you can ask her to call me in."

"Yao, I told you, they want whole turkeys, not just the tails."

"Whole turkeys it will be!"

"Please, don't tell me how you're going to do it--I don't want to know."

Madame Long Neck was thrilled. Long Neck smelled a rat.

"If these are American turkeys, what brand are they?" he asked.

Long Neck was surprised when Yao gave him the name and address of a firm on Maryland's Eastern Shore. A call to his Commercial Officer confirmed that it did, in fact, exist.

"All right, but payment on delivery," was his grudging assent. Yao assured him that they would do business together for years to come.

Kojo accompanied Yao to the wrought-iron gate.

"Monday is your day off, isn't it?" asked Yao. "Come to the farm bright and early. I'll need your help if we're going to get all those turkeys to Madame Long Neck by Wednesday."

Shortly before dawn on Monday, Kojo arrived at Yao's farm to find it already alive with activity. Yao's wife and children and nephews and nieces had already begun to drag turkeys out of the enclosure and the first head fell to machete blows as he made his way inside.

"These turkeys look nice and plump," he said to Yao as the morning breeze swirled feathers in the air. "I've never seen this breed before. They don't look like the scrawny ones you usually see in the market."

"You thought I was lying to Long Neck, didn't you?" Yao replied. "Well, these birds are American. Not born in America, but an American breed I picked up from a poultry-raising project a while back. Even if they wanted Rhode Island Reds, I can get them! We're wasting time. Take this."

"Kojo took the butcher knife and sat down and began sharpening it against a stone already worn smooth by previous rubbings.

"You know how they cut their birds before they put them in plastic. Show us exactly how they do it."

"Do you think that will be enough to fool them?"

"Look." Yao pointed across the compound where the bright daylight was beginning to shine. One of his daughters was carefully peeling one red-and-white paper label after another off a wet stack and laying them in the sun to dry.

"Enyonam, the big market lady, buys crates full of boxes of frozen turkey tails from the importer at his freezer. Then, she sells them box by box to the ladies who cook and sell them on the street. Each box has a label or two in it with the name of the American company on it. They gave me their labels and, in return, I'll give them the heads and feet and livers to cook up."

"How are you going to freeze them?"

"Easy. When we finish butchering, we'll put them in plastic bags with the labels on the outside and take them to the importer. He liked my idea. We'll freeze them overnight in his locker before we deliver them to Madame Long Neck. We'll give him the tails and the wings for his trouble."

Kojo had been a reluctant participant in the project but now he was overcome with admiration for Yao's cleverness and enterprise. His face lit up with a grin and he approached his first turkey with enthusiasm.

Kojo's hands were sore and raw by the time the last load of turkeys left for their cold destination in the back of a beat-up little Renault taxi. The washing of the concrete floors of the compound and the burning of the turkey feathers still had not rid the place of flies. Exhausted, he leaned against the wall, too tired to swat the swarms of mosquitoes that began replacing the flies with the setting of the sun.

On Wednesday morning, the same decrepit taxi ferried loads of frozen turkeys from the importer's locker to the freezers at Long Neck's residence. Madame Long Neck was delighted and for the next twenty-four hours had more to do than in the preceding year. There was extra help to order around. Plates of a quivering red jelly went into the refrigerators. Sweet potatoes were covered with a sweet syrup that would make them inedible to any of Kojo's compatriots. Kojo supervised a team that tore fresh bread into bits and dried them in the oven, while remembering his own breakfast of day-old bread dipped in watery sweet hot cocoa. The corn to be boiled or roasted was the only part of the upcoming feast that was recognizable. American sweet corn can't grow in tropical Africa, however, so the celebrants would have to be content with the chewier but no less tasty local field corn. The turkeys received Madame Long Neck's personal and devoted attention.

The day of the great feast, Yao arrived bedecked in a brilliant white flowing *boubou* with matching cap and shoes. He circulated among the celebrators to elicit their opinion of his birds.

Madame Long Neck was gushing.

"Mr. Yao, you certainly saved the day with your American turkeys. There would be no Thanksgiving without you."

"It is my pleasure to be of service to you," he replied with a bow, before Madame Long Neck rushed off leaving him in the company of two wives of diplomats.

"Your turkey is very tasty, Mr. Yao," said the first as she bent over to pick turkey meat from between the teeth of her freckle-faced son. "But I'm afraid it's little firmer than what we're used to."

Her companion was a younger, bravely stylish woman. Her panty-hose and sweat-streaked make-up in the sweltering heat and stifling humidity attested to her determination to remain chic and fashionable during the purgatory of a two-year tour in the "White Man's Graveyard" before returning to more hospitable climes.

"Of course," she rejoined condescendingly as if to a country cousin, "people are eating poultry that way now. It's so much healthier and less fattening."

Yao really didn't know why it was such a good thing not to be fat, but he smiled and mentally filed away her endorsement for future reference.

In late afternoon, the day's festivities were interrupted when Long Neck stepped up to a microphone and tapped for attention. The crowd gathered around him, silent except for the occasional whine of a child and turkey gobbles from some of the younger Volunteers in the back rows. Long Neck read the proclamation of the President of the United States to the American people on the occasion of Thanksgiving. In many ways, it was the same as in the preceding years, but Yao didn't know it and listened more intently than the rest of the crowd. The references to Pilgrims and Indians and harvests gave presidential confirmation to the tales that Madame Long Neck had recounted to Kojo. It was still a puzzle, however, as to why the Indians would plant perfectly good and edible fish with their corn. By the time that Long Neck came to the part about famine in Africa, the crowd was restless. The few who had been listening had turned their thoughts elsewhere or engaged in the discreet buzz of conversation that began to compete with Long Neck's thin voice. Yao strained to hear every word about how the American people were moved to help end hunger around the world.

As the ceremony came to an end and the group dispersed, Yao found himself near two middle-aged men in Bermuda shorts.

"Say," said one, "on the way down from the mine yesterday I must have seen three of your grain trucks dumped by the side of the road--all that corn and sorghum with the "American flag and handshake" label on the sacks, just sittin' there waitin' for the next rain. It's a damned shame. Don't those boys from up there in famine country know how to drive?"

"I don't know," sighed the second. "It's so stupid. They pull over to the side of the road to pee or something and the shoulder of the road just collapses under the weight of the truck. It's bad enough to have to wait for the stuff to arrive in port."

Yao could not restrain himself.

"Tell me something," he asked. "Instead of bringing grain all the way from America to send up to the famine countries, why don't you just buy grain from us here, where there is no famine? We can produce enough, we're much closer to them--surely it would be cheaper."

The man looked at Yao with condescending exasperation. The last thing he wanted to do on his Thanksgiving was to explain the rude facts of economic life to another naïve "local." He would have excused himself quickly, but after all, he owed something to the "Man Who Saved Thanksgiving."

"Mr. Yao, it's really very simple. America has grain--lots of corn, wheat, sorghum, millet, and rice--more than we can ever use ourselves. To keep up the price for our farmers, the government buys up large quantities of grain and stores it. It's part of this stock that we use to meet our obligations to famine victims. At the same time, people get a chance to see what American agriculture can provide. Marketing is what we call it. There's more and more American rice and wheat on the market here, haven't you noticed? Bread is now cheaper than your traditional corn porridge or your yam *foufou*. We sell you high-quality rice at a price cheaper than you can hope to produce it. So it's really not in our interest to buy grain here, is it? Besides, at the rate that the Sahara is heading your way, you'd be better advised to stock up yourselves!"

The two slapped Yao on the back, thanked him for his turkeys, and left to retrieve their families.

In the meantime, Long Neck and Madame had positioned themselves on the walkway just inside the gate, signaling to the crowd that it was time to leave. Yao entered the line that had quickly formed.

"Oh, Mr. Yao, I just don't know how to thank you," said Madame Long Neck when she came to him. "I suppose that I should ask you right now if you could supply us with hot dogs and buns for our Fourth of July picnic!"

Yao's interest was piqued at the prospect of another deal.

"What's a hot dog?" he asked.

"Well, they're a kind of sausage," replied Madame as Long Neck reached for Yao's hand. Yao remembered the "diplomatic handshake" too late and all at once found himself standing on the pavement outside Long Neck's compound. Madame's voice continued faintly above the hubbub of the departing crowd.

"We put mustard and relish on them," she cried.

The dry desert wind called the *Harmattan* was just beginning to reach the coast with its load of fine white dust. It billowed Yao's *boubou* as he strode toward the crossroads bus stop, intently pondering the new mystery of hot dogs. Kojo would have some explaining to do.

A HUSBAND SO NICE

I didn't believe Jeannette when she said she was going to Paris. The "Ghana Girls" who frequented the bars of this West African port changed their fantasies as often as they changed their names, and that was often enough. Jeannette had been Akossiwa, she had been Maggie and Comfort and Janet. Now, having replaced her pidgin English with French learned from the radio and from the open-air cinema, she was Jeannette.

"*Fovi*, dash me t'ousand flancs," she bubbled as she hurried through my door early one Sunday morning. "I go for Accra, go get visa for Paris!"

Sunday is my sleep-in morning so I didn't argue with her and complied with an indulgent smile. She had proved her generosity often in years past. After the night clubs closed, bartenders, "Ghana Girls," musicians, taxi drivers, and an occasional non-affluent expatriate like me would end up at the "Paris Snack" on rickety chairs in front of greasy omelets with Zaïrian music blaring with pops and squeaks from the speakers. When the money ran out, Jeannette would go off to "wake up an old Swiss man" and return with a few thousand francs to keep the party going. I couldn't begrudge her taxi money to the Ghanaian capital, and went back to sleep.

A month later, I went by Jeannette's house. The huge concrete block building was home to dozens of people. Clothing hung from open doors, fans fought a losing battle with the stifling heat, and the smells of charcoal smoke, cooking fat, and hot pepper wafted inside from the back steps.

"Jeannette dey?" I asked a young taxi driver.

"She go for Paris."

"No be so!"

"E be so. You know dis girl, Carlotta? 'er boyfriend, French boy Jean-Paul. 'e go home for Paris, take 'am bot'!"

Jean-Paul worked for a French company in Ghana and frequently came over to visit Carlotta, who was "tight friends" with Jeannette. On those occasions, the four of us would sometimes go to the cinema and later to the night clubs. He was small, excruciatingly thin, with a beak of a nose and hollow, sunken cheeks. He chain-smoked Gauloises . I spoke to him in English and he unfailingly responded in French.

Just how tight Jeannette was with Carlotta I had found out early on. I dropped by the "Paris Snack" one morning for a beer after a dusty ride into town. Carlotta was there visiting Blackie, a dark toothless girl who worked out of one of the straw-mattress rooms in the back.

"Who's your seamstress?" I asked as she slipped a new dress over her enormous breasts and down over her skinny legs.

"Jeannette," she replied. "She dash me dis dress."

"That's very nice of her."

"She like me," said Carlotta with a shrug.

Blackie went into hysterics and punched Carlotta's arm as if trying to pry something more out of her. Carlotta relented with an embarrassed grin.

"Jeannette love me."

I contemplated Jeannette and Carlotta together with a mixture of sympathy and titillation. Jeannette was short and muscular, pretty and slim but for her ample African hips. I imagined her to be the ardent one, the aggressor. She would go after Carlotta with the same frenzied concentration that she applied to doing a lascivious Watusi on the dance floor of the Rêve Night Club while potential dates looked on behind a haze of smoke. Carlotta was tall and thin, languid, and passive. She was amused and somewhat puzzled, yet grateful, for the attention that so many men and more than a few women paid to her large, firm breasts. Carlotta, I imagined, would receive Jeannette's insistent attentions with playful and affectionate resistance but would eventually give way. The thought of their sweat-slickened bodies writhing together tortured my imagination on solitary nights in the village. My reverie was always brought up short by the realization that they were friends and that their passion would be real and not feigned as it was with their night club dates.

Reality and not fantasy had brought Jeannette and Carlotta to town from their thatch-roof homes in rural villages. They had spent little time in the tin-roofed schoolhouses. That privilege was reserved for their brothers.

Jeannette had watched her mother and saw the life that awaited her. She would rear children, suckling them at her breast until the age of two. She would grow food by hoeing scattered patches of farm and garden. She would gather firewood at increasing distances from home and carry it back in bundles on her head. She would draw water from the stream or, if she was lucky, from a well.

All these tasks were women's work that she would have readily accepted. She came to realize, however, that the life that awaited her would be even harder than that of her mother. Her long-suffering mother was as incapable of bitterness as she was of comprehension of the growing inequities she faced in her daily life.

"In the old days," she told Jeannette, "life was hard, yes, but we all did our part. Men used to be warriors, but what war is there now? Nothing but fights about land. They spend years arguing, all for nothing.

"They used to be hunters," she continued, "but what is there left to hunt? Nothing. Clear new fields? Where will they find new fields now? We're too many! Even our houses, made with cement blocks and tin roofs, they take money and money is what we don't have."

"They could help the women," Jeannette had suggested. They shared the thought of the men doing women's work with peals of laughter.

City life held out the promise of stylish clothes, movies of far-off places, dancing till dawn in night clubs, learning a trade, earning money, and even finding a rich husband.

Jeannette's inability to bear a child had finally caused her to leave home. Try as she might, she could not prove her fertility to potential husbands by having a first child. The local diviner tossed his white cowrie shells repeatedly on smooth sand with the same result.

"Someone in the village has cast a spell on you to avenge his family's honor," he said, "for something that happened in the time of your grandfather. If you stay, you will never conceive."

Her mother helped her to steal away to the city. Helping her daughter to escape was her only little victory in life, from which she rationed herself quiet moments of satisfaction for years to follow.

Jeannette had been lying beside me at the swimming pool of the city's largest hotel as she told me of the diviner's warning. She brimmed with confidence in his diagnosis. She seemed convinced that with a little more persistence she would have her wish, in spite of the fact that she was still barren after several years in the city.

"I dey go *Mammy Wata* man," she said.

The cult of the mermaid, *Mammy Wata*, thrives up and down the coast, its believers seeking wealth or fertility. Usually, one was at the expense of the other in the cult's order of things.

"What did you do?" I asked.

"I take 'am chickens an' money an' t'ings," she replied. "E take me to forest, wash me naked in holy water. Den we take t'ings, put in white cloth, make an' go t'ro in ocean for *Mammy Wata*."

"What kind of things?" I asked.

"Can't tell," she laughed.

We stared at the variety of shapes, sizes, and colors of tourists and traveling businessmen who mixed with the local African elite and resident expatriates around the pool. The skinny French women competed for male attention with the more modestly undressed but more voluptuous African women by stripping to their standard pool attire: stiletto-heel sandals, a thin gold ankle bracelet, a bikini bottom pulled up between the buttocks to leave only a *de facto* G-string, and a look of bored indifference.

I poked lightly at the scar that emerged from her bikini bottom, moved north to her navel, and then struck out due east and west.

"What's that?"

"Dey cut me."

"Why?"

"Don' know," she replied with a shrug. "Was pickin'--small girl. Get sick. Dey took me for hospital, cut me."

I couldn't bring myself to question her further. Could the amoebic dysentery so common in the villages have done what it so often does: escape into the abdominal cavity and attack an organ such as the liver, or the ovaries? The doctor's skill had probably saved her life. Like *Mammy Wata*, did it require its beneficiary to sacrifice something valuable in exchange?

Counterattacking in the battle for poolside attention, Jeannette rolled over on her stomach with a laugh. As she bared her buttocks, male heads turned in unison.

"White girls got no bottom, no *nyansh*," she announced triumphantly as she arched her own into the air.

As the years went by, I liked to think that Jeannette's dreams had come true in Paris. It eased my conscience to see or imagine old friends succeeding. My forays into the city from my thatch-roof adobe house up-country were long ago replaced by forays up-country from my air-conditioned house in the capital. Presumably, my experience and technical expertise justified my changed station in life.

I was thankful that I didn't miss running into Jeannette at the airport a few months ago. I was leaving for a month and she had just arrived for a month's visit, so we piled into the airport bar with her family and friends. Alternating between her own language, Éwé, pidgin English, and breathless Parisian French, she regaled us with descriptions of her life--her dress shop, her home, and especially her French husband, Thierry. Her '70s Afro wig had been replaced by elegant, intricate braids. Perfume hung tantalizingly in the air. Thierry had a good position and treated her like a queen. His parents accepted her without hesitation and spoiled her like a favorite daughter. Paris had not disappointed her.

"Really," she said, looking dreamily upward and giving out a thoroughly French sigh, "I never thought I would find a husband so nice."

We toasted Jeannette's happiness before I had to catch my plane. The long trip had been made easier and I awoke from dozing with a smile on my face.

Jeannette had found Paris, but in all my years of traveling between Africa and the United States, I had never gotten closer than the transit lounge of Charles de Gaulle Airport. My opportunity finally came when I stopped off for a day on the way to New York. My host was a French official who was involved in publishing a manual that I had written. Our morning meeting went well and he invited me to a late lunch before my evening departure. He was very curious about Africa where he was soon to visit for the first time.

"You have an African wife?"

"Yes, I do."

"I have heard," he said, unable to restrain himself, "that when visiting in Africa, your host insists on offering you his wife for the night!"

"Not his wife," I replied with a patronizing smile. "His sister, perhaps, but not his wife."

He missed the sarcasm of my reply and was happy to have his information corrected.

We left the restaurant in late afternoon and sped through traffic.

"Before you leave," he chuckled, "I'll give you a last little glimpse of Africa."

He detoured through the *Bois de Boulogne*, the huge urban park. Suddenly, he pulled to the curb at a spot where black prostitutes congregated under the watchful eyes of their pimps.

The nearest one rushed to my window. I looked up and Jeannette and I found ourselves staring at each other, unable to speak. As I rushed to roll down my window, I recognized behind her a familiar hawk-nosed figure sucking on a Gauloise and an equally familiar top-heavy figure teetering on thin legs and spike heels.

"*Fovi,*" she said finally with a dry laugh from her throat, "I never thought I would find a husband so nice."

TASK ANALYSIS

Dear Boss,

Before I begin to fill out this form that you have given to us, let me say first what an excellent form it is. May I have an extra one? I know we shouldn't waste paper, but I do want to encourage my youngest. I'd like to show him what he can do if he would just apply himself. Why, only yesterday he came home from school with his right hand swollen to the size of a coconut. Do you know why? Well, no matter how many times his schoolmaster hit his hand with a ruler to punish him, he still gave wrong answers. Can you believe it?

All of my other children at least finished sixth grade, even though none passed their Certificate Test. My daughter made it to secondary school for a while, until someone made her pregnant. She said it was one of her classmates, some boy in short pants, but I don't believe it. It was probably one of the teachers but she won't tell the truth. What can a poor man do? My youngest is as dumb as a clay water pot. It's the burden God has given me to carry and I can only accept.

When I heard that one of our young countrymen who had gone off to America to learn the new science of management had come home to join our department, I can't tell you how proud I was. Science is hard enough. No one likes to take it in school if they can avoid it. But a new science! That's impressive. You finished on time, too. So many others, they dawdle and make excuses to stay there. Some don't come home at all. You know the ones that I mean.

I'm not surprised that the Director-General gave you the job of making our department work better. Who better to do it? We're the biggest department, after all. We are the ones who serve our valiant peasant farmers, like the President says. I know you've been hard at work with our other bosses to get things ready. Who do you suppose takes down the papers you tape to the walls? Me! I try to do a good job and not pull the paint off. I'm sure that what you're doing is what we need.

We're very disorganized and we waste time. Why, just think about all the greeting that goes on when the staff arrives in the morning. Everyone has to greet everyone and ask about the health of everyone in their family, from their grandmother down to the last pot and pan in the kitchen! By the time they're done, the ladies have come around selling beans and rice and tapioca for the mid-morning break.

I was surprised that you asked me, of all people, to participate in your task analysis. And Yao and the other drivers and young Miss Akossiwa, the apprentice typist who goes home with with old Mr. Agbévivinto the accountant. No one has ever asked me what I thought about anything, especially about my job. So it is with great pleasure that I now fill out your form.

Ministry of Rural Development
Department of Extension Services
Human Resource Management Rationalization Program
Employee Task Analysis Sheet

Position: *Janitor (formerly Field Agent at the Yéyékopé office of the Upper Valley District)*

Employee Name: *Amékuku Mu-adzé Mensah (a.k.a. Kwami Kolegbè--I don't really have a long neck like a goose but they call me Kolegbè anyway)*

Description of task	Frequency	Knowledge and skills required to perform the task
I clean all the offices in the building, beginning very early--about 5:30 a.m.	*Once a day*	*Thanks to the solid upbringing I received at home from my elder brothers, I manage to do this work without dwelling on my humble station in life.*
I dust all the furniture: tables, chairs, cabinets, windows, and even the pictures on the walls.	*Once a day*	*It is a sin against Man and God for someone who knows how to do a good job to do a bad job .*
I wash the hand towels for the rest rooms	*Once a week*	*Cleanliness and all life itself depends on water.*

Description of task	Frequency	Knowledge and skills required to perform the task
I mop the floor of the front porch, the main hallway, the reception area, all the offices, and the secretarial pool.	*Once a week*	*Given all the effort I put out, I have never once been reprimanded by the Director-General. This is my supreme wish: I always want to do a good job so that I will never be reprimanded.*
I remove the cobwebs in the corners and near the ceilings of each office.	*Once every two weeks*	*I cannot neglect this task any more than I could neglect the house where I have found lodging, or my own house.*
Janitor: that's what I am. Everyone is my Master. I go to the post office to get the mail and to send letters.	*Each day, at no special time*	*Conscientiously, without sadness or melancholy, I do my job. In my heart, I know that it is not my fault that I am no longer a field agent.*

Description of task	Frequency	Knowledge and skills required to perform the task
After wiping off the desks, I am very careful to arrange everything in order--pens, pencils, books, and paper--each thing in its proper place.	*Once a day (Twice a day in the Director-General's office)*	*If the desks are neat and everything is in its place, visitors notice right away that the person who works in this office is well-organized. That can help give all of our office a good reputation.*
At this early hour of the morning, while wiping the windows, I am very careful not to let mosquitoes get in the offices.	*Every morning*	*I learned this from experience. The staff would be very unhappy to come to work and find their offices full of mosquitoes. Sometimes they hide under the desks and bite the staff on the ankles!*
I empty the wastebaskets of torn and ripped and useless papers.	*Every morning and afternoon*	*Work is everything. Work is the law.*

Description of task	Frequency	Knowledge and skills required to perform the task
After my morning tasks from 5:30 to 7:00 a.m., I look like a prisoner who has just escaped from prison. From the first day, I realized that I would get dirty doing this work, so I keep my toilet articles out back where I go to shower. There, I return in my most primitive condition.	*Every morning*	*As the saying goes: after the rain, the sunny days will follow. Man is born on one of these bad days. He is destined to suffer and to come to understand certain things in life, and then to die. So, I don't worry.*
A janitor does all the cleaning work of a government office. It should be temporary work, a first step up the career ladder because it's truly difficult and requires great patience.		*One has to know the world and life to be able to adapt to it. It takes experience, courage, and patience to do the janitor's job.*

Description of task	Frequency	Knowledge and skills required to perform the task
It sometimes happens that someone will say to me:"go to the bank" and then someone else says:"go get such-and-such for me someplace," and without even giving me a chance to finish the second task the first one wants to know if his task is done!	*From time to time*	*Who can judge his neighbor? Only God. A French saying goes, "This can only happen to the living." Good or bad, I accept my fate, my destiny. When they replaced me with a boy who is younger and has more education, I could only accept and not doubt their intentions.*
I am willing to do the job of janitor and I do it as best I can. The problems I have encountered in life obligate me to do it.		*No matter what their strengths and weaknesses, no child of mine will ever do this job while I'm alive. I say this in all humility and without conceit.*

\

CHANGE OF NAME

Every office should have someone like Niiquah. He's always telling a joke or teasing, making the long, boring, tiresome day of shuffling papers and tallying sums go faster. He's a good worker and isn't distracted easily from the task at hand, although you wouldn't guess it from all the chatter emanating from his desk.

We look forward to his arrival each morning at our offices on the second floor of the Ghana International Bank of Trade, Industry, and Credit in Accra.

"*Graphic* here?" he invariably inquires before making the rounds of every desk in the office to greet us individually. Niiquah's job is different. He verifies the bookkeeping entries of transaction operations, so he arrives an hour later and leaves an hour later than the rest of us.

The *Graphic* in question is one of our oldest daily tabloids, *The Daily Graphic*. Like an alcoholic and his spirits, Niiquah can hardly make it through the day without his dose of *Graphic*. He is not a great student of current affairs. Neither the articles nor the editorial comments interest him. Niiquah's window on the Ghanaian world, his finger on the pulse of our country, is the adverts. They fascinate and delight him, and none arouses his spirit more than the boxes near the back entitled "Change of Name."

"It's a big decision," he would say, "to change one's name."

"Listen to this: 'I, Miss Grace Owusu, of Memorial Secretarial College at Kokomlemle, Accra, wish to be known and called Mrs. Comfort Grace Mensah. All documents bearing my former name still valid.' Our lady is changing her name because she has gotten married. What greater change than that? Congratulations and best wishes to her." He then launched into a discourse on the importance of marriage and the family to our society.

Hardly a day passed when a "Change of Name" did not provoke an amusing foray into his vivid imagination or the recounting of a little morality play.

"What's this?" he read. "'I, Mrs. Matilda Wilhelmina Boateng of Ibero-African Trans-Shipping Corporation, Tema, wish to be called Miss Adolphina Osei. All former documents . . .etc.' Did Mr. B turn to drink and abuse this gentle lady? Was he a poor provider? Or perhaps our lady was angered when her husband chose to take a second wife? Our mothers accepted polygamy and even found some solace and solidarity in it. Times have changed and the young ones want to be the only wife. Perhaps she became a shrew and a harridan after she was married, and made her poor husband miserable with her unreasonable demands."

Niiquah seemed lost in thought for a few moments. He advanced a final reflection before returning to his sums.

"I wonder which is preferable: for a man to have several wives, all of them and their children recognized as his legitimate family, or for a man to have one wife and family at home and his mistresses and children outside?"

"Religion can bring about a change of name," he observed one day. "'I, George Percival Jasper Tetteh, of State Refrigerated Container Corporation at Takoradi, wish to be known and called Muhammad Issifu Abdel-Aziz.' Our friend will be off to Mecca one of these days. When he gets back, there will be another 'Change' so that he can insert 'AlHaji' in front of his name."

"For some, a new name is advertising for business," Niiquah said another day. "Listen to this: 'I, Prince Reuben Acquah, soothsayer and healer at Three Corner Junction, Ashanti Region, first African to combine the Eastern Arts of Tarot, Numerology, Phrenology, and Palmistry with our Traditional African Practices of Fâ and Herbal Medicine, wish to be known and called Bishop Jesus Krishna Buddha. All former documents remain valid.'"

Niiquah mused, "Did Jesus, Krishna, and Buddha have as much difficulty in getting their documents as the average Ghanaian?"

"The Ouédraogo whose family is from Burkina and the Lossos in the Army and the Cotokoli traders were all born and raised in Ghana," he said. "Ghanaian names make them feel more secure in their adopted homeland."

Some changes were flights of sheer fancy. How many Elvises were there? Even Niiquah lost count. "King Alexander Darius Solomon" graced new documents, as did names of revolutionary solidarity adopted by some of our brothers freshly arrived from studies in Eastern Bloc countries: Lumumba, Stokely, Ché, Eduardo Mondlane, Mandela, and more.

Every day the "Name Change Parade" continued and Niiquah never failed to make us laugh. Sometimes he made us think.

Niiquah's attention, however, was not limited to the "Change of Name" announcements.

"Look at this," he exclaimed one day as he threw the newspaper on the desk in front of him. "'Appearing now through the end of the month at the Ballroom of the Côte d'Azure Beach Club Hotel, Sexy Suzy and Her

Sensational Breasts: Exotic European Lady Striptease Artiste.'"

He turned the page.

"And now look at this announcement: 'Saturday Night at the Ace of Spades Night Club: Amateur Breast Contest--Cash Prizes for the Best Breasts in Accra.' The Europeans' breast obsession is to be ours as well."

He shook his head and thought for a few moments.

"I have an idea," he said finally. "I think that Auntie Akosua should enter the Breast Contest!"

The sound of a chair scraping on the floor pierced the room. Auntie Akosua reacted immediately and decisively to the mention of her name in this way. She pushed the chair back from her desk in the far corner of the room and rose to her feet.

Niiquah talked quickly as Auntie Akosua moved out from behind her desk with her fists clenched at her sides and began walking toward him. She was not amused.

"Who better to represent the best of Ghanaian womanhood," he continued, "than a woman who has been a hard-working and valued employee of this bank for many years and, at the same time, has been a good wife and has suckled at her breast six wonderful children who will contribute mightily to our country's future?"

By the time Auntie Akosua reached Niiquah's desk, he had redeemed himself with his speech. She could not be angry with someone who praised her children. Her irritation had given way to satisfaction that she could barely conceal.

"Foolish boy," she said and gave Niiquah a playful cuff to the side of the head before returning to her desk.

I asked Niiquah once how he had come to be so interested in name changes.

"I changed my own name," he replied to my surprise. "Not once, but twice. Niiquah was the name that my family gave me--a perfectly good Ghanaian name. The farther I went in my studies, the more I identified the good things in life with the Europeans. I wanted to be like them, so I fashioned my own name--Chesley Winston Rockford. The names have no significance whatsoever, other than the fact that they are European."

"What made you take back your old name?" I asked.

"My 'new clothes' never did fit me very well," he answered. "Then something happened that made me stop and think about my life. It was the late 1960s. I would catch our local Bedford 'Mammy Wagon' into the lorry park and cut through to Liberty Avenue to walk to the Bank. Every day, down below Kingsway, I would encounter these young men on the street who would harangue me, politely but insistently."

"Some mad market-dwellers," I laughed.

"To the contrary," he replied seriously. "They were anything but mad. These were educated men, but they refused anything European in their dress or speech. They wore only country cloth and carried a goatskin bag. They used our language eloquently, like the old men in the villages, with no borrowed words from English or Portuguese. They asked me, 'Brother, why do you imitate them? Are not your own culture and your own language good enough for you?'"

"I fended them off with good humor but what they said was eating away at me. Sometimes I would wake up at night in a cold sweat. Does trying to be modern and progressive mean being more European and less Ghanaian? Do the values that I grew up with mean anything now, or are they to be discarded as easily as I discarded my former name? I decided that I wouldn't surrender so eagerly. I decided to try to be African and modern, and to take back my old name and be proud of it."

"Make no mistake about it," he concluded. "We Ghanaians are no longer behaving like Ghanaians. We started so proudly. Now our neighbors delight in seeing how the mighty have fallen. We're as known for our crooks and our prostitutes as for our gold and our cocoa. We need a moral revolution in this country."

We're doing better now in Ghana, even though the Whiteman is punishing us unmercifully with his Structural Adjustment Programme. In those dark days at the beginning of the decade of the 1980s, however, it was hard to be moral, let alone revolutionary. Our proud *cedi* that had once equaled the US dollar had become practically worthless--the laughingstock of currencies. Luxuries had disappeared from the shelves of the shops. In the markets, the necessities of life had become so rare that they commanded a king's ransom. The breweries were closed. We schemed to possess the pitiful little CFA francs to cross the nearest border and buy our own Ghanaian matches, toilet roll, and bread.

We all had to sell something to supplement our worthless salaries. In my case, the only thing I had to sell was paper. A paper from the bank--made to look very legal and proper--was helpful to some foreign business people who sought my acquaintance. I didn't like to do it, but like everyone else, I had to use my wits. In return, I could cross the border to their cousins' store and, with a chit from them, buy things to consume and to re-sell. In the office, we didn't judge each other. Each of us did what he thought was necessary in order to survive. Each of us had his own little deal.

Each one except Niiquah. He said nothing of our deals. He struggled to farm and to sell the meager produce rather than emulate our compromises. His fields were far from town and transport disappeared with the evaporating petrol. He became less animated. He looked tired and haggard.

Then one day he collapsed unconscious at his desk. A less fortunate man might have died, but our Managing Director, perhaps fearing a tarnished image for the Bank, stepped into the breach. His Mercedes burned precious petrol to transport Niiquah to the clinic, where he received the fluid and nourishment he needed through a tube.

He had not eaten and had drunk only water for several days, preferring to deprive himself rather than his family.

It was several weeks before Niiquah returned to the Bank. We greeted him heartily but respected his desire to limit the fanfare and return to the normal routine as expeditiously as possible. The *Graphic*, that had become rare due to paper shortages, reappeared on the scene in a slimmed-down edition as if to honor its most diligent reader's return. Niiquah opened the *Graphic* and as usual went straight to the "Change of Name" adverts and began reading the first one aloud.

"I," he said. He slowed as he read my name. "Timothy Peterson of Ghana International Bank of Trade, Industry, and Credit, Accra, wish henceforth to be known as Kojo Akakpo Mawulawe. All former documents valid."

"It means 'God will provide' in our Éwé language," I explained.

Just then, there was a knock at the door and Niiquah rose to answer it. I could hear my foreign friends ask for me.

"Timothy Peterson?" said Niiquah, repeating my former name. "I'm sorry. No one by that name works here any more."

He closed the door and sat down at his desk. A broad smile covered his face.

People's Daily
GRAPHIC

CHICKEN GEORGE

"I am the original 'Chicken George!'"

"You are not, you old fool."

"Then who is?"

"Alex Haley wrote about his ancestor, 'Chicken George,' in **Roots**. You know that."

"But I was 'Chicken George' here in Accra long before Haley ever thought of writing **Roots**."

"Well, Haley's 'Chicken George' was 'Chicken George' long before you ever set foot in Accra."

"That may be true, but Haley's 'Chicken George' didn't bring Southern Fried Chicken to Accra, did he? I did. That makes me the original 'Chicken George' in this town."

"No, it doesn't, Kunta Kintay. That makes you the original Colonel Sanders in this town."

The banter between George and his wife, Lucinda, was always like this.

People came to expect it and enjoy it. If they left "Chicken George's Afro-American Restaurant" without it, they weren't entirely satisfied, no matter how good the food was.

Promise and Wanda giggled as they ate their chicken. George and Lucinda were as much a part of a sick Peace Corps Volunteer's care as the medicines dispensed at the Medical Office. At least, this was true for the few who were lucky enough to be lodged at the restaurant in rooms that Peace Corps had rented for Volunteers recovering from illness.

"Promise is such a pretty name," said Lucinda. "Does it have a special meaning? Is it a family name?"

"Actually, my folks are Sixties people," replied Promise. "I got a Sixties flower-child name. They were Peace Corps Volunteers here in Ghana. I was born right here in Accra."

"You don't say!" exclaimed George.

"When Ghanaians see my birthplace on my passport, or ask me where I was born," said Promise, "it really causes quite a stir."

It wasn't long before George and Lucinda determined that they had met Promise's parents on several occasions and they reminisced about the old days.

"Yes," said George. "We were some of the very first Afros in Ghana. Afros is what we called ourselves. When Kwame Nkrumah invited his Afro-American brothers and sisters to come home and help build the nation, we were in the first wave!"

"Yes, we were, Dear," said Lucinda. Her tone had changed. She was no longer teasing and combative. She placed her hand on his to comfort him.

She knew that reminiscing about the old days eventually made him very emotional and she could hear the beginnings of strain in his voice.

"Kwame Nkrumah was a great, great man," George continued. "He was the greatest black man who ever lived, which doesn't take anything away from Martin or Malcolm. He called us back to the Motherland and we came."

"Have many of the other Afros stayed?" inquired Wanda gently. "I know Ghana went through periods when things were very hard--much harder than they are today. Did many go home--I mean, back to the States--during those times?"

"Yes, many went back," replied George. "It was rough after Nkrumah was overthrown. Then Busia came to power and kicked hundreds of thousands of his fellow Africans out of the country. It was a terrible, shameful thing to do. Some of the Afros got caught up in that fiasco and were cheated out of their businesses and their possessions. I don't think that they've ever gotten over feeling so betrayed. A few years ago, back in the early eighties, things were very difficult, too. By then, Ghana had fallen so low. It was hard to stay in business and survive, even for those of us who wanted most to stay. It's hard to be 'Chicken George' without chickens! But through all the hard times, many of us Afros stayed. Stick around this place long enough and you'll meet some of the others."

Promise noticed that Wanda's mood seem to darken slightly as the conversation progressed. She waited until George and Lucinda had retired for the night before speaking.

"What's the matter, Wanda?" asked Promise. "Are you feeling bad?"

"It's ironic," she replied. "You're a white girl and yet, you've got an automatic connection to Ghana--you're a Sister, after all!"

"As for me," she continued, "I'm black, but I'm kind of confused and unsure. A lot of the time, I feel very comfortable here in Ghana--like I belong, like I'm at home. People are so nice to me, so hospitable. Other times, I feel like I'm from another planet. Some Ghanaians seem to think that because I'm black like them, that I must automatically act like them, think like them, that I automatically speak Twi like them ... I'm trying to keep learning, believe me, but sometimes I get so frustrated with them and they get pretty frustrated with me!"

"Sounds like a marriage, or at least a boyfriend," Promise joked.

"Yeah, you're right about that," said Wanda as a smile returned to her face. "I guess that's the main thing in all relationships; you gotta work on 'em. Nothing is automatic."

As they crossed the garden to return to their rooms, Promise nodded toward Lucinda and George's house and spoke quietly.

"Do you see that portrait on the wall of their living room? It's a young man in an Army officer's uniform. Seems a bit old. The uniform's not American--it looks Ghanaian, I think."

"I wonder who it is," Wanda said as they said their good-nights.

When Wanda and Promise returned to the restaurant the next day after a morning at the Medical Office, George and Lucinda were sitting on a sofa in the courtyard with a man that the two had not yet met. Tall, thin, and muscular, his hairline was receding and what hair remained was salt-and-pepper. He wore a sleeveless *batakali* shirt, shorts, and truck-tire sandals. His bicycle was leaned against the wall behind him.

"I told you," George yelled out to them, "that you would meet some more of the original Afros around here if you stayed long enough. Come over here and meet someone."

"Meet James," said George.

Before he could continue, Promise interrupted.

"So you're James," she said. "You're a farmer, aren't you?"

"Yes, that would be me," he replied with a bemused smile.

"My Mom and Dad talked about you. They said that you have a farm where you grow corn and raise chickens," Promise continued. "They said that you write poetry, too. I'm so glad to meet you."

Quietly and unobtrusively, and without a hint of self-righteousness, James had long ago engaged with the spiritual side of Ghana and Ghanaians. Working the soil, growing corn and vegetables, raising chickens, practicing traditional methods that he carefully and conservatively married to some modern techniques that he brought with him--James felt that he was trodding the soil of his ancestors and at the same time he found a way to make a modest but steady living. He bred the bigger American chickens with the more disease-resistant Ghanaian ones. His farm was not enormous but he helped keep "Chicken George's" supplied with chickens and eggs. At the end of each month, James made his way to the cashier's window at the U.S. Embassy to pick up a small but helpful military disability retirement check from his time in the U.S. Navy and occasionally continued on to the Embassy Medical Unit.

James' poetry appeared regularly in small literary magazines in West Africa and the United States that paid for his writings only with free copies. They could be found occasionally in the Saturday edition of one of Ghana's tabloid newspapers. Self-published paperback collections of his poems gathered dust in Accra's bookshops and in the gift shops of tourist hotels. At the beginning of the nineties, however, James' gentle poetry emerged in African and African-American literary and intellectual circles as a counterpoint to the writings of the "Afro-pessimists." In particular, they were an alternative to some of the more vehement works of some African-American journalists and scholars. These writers despaired of Africa's tragic conflicts and gave vent to the simmering resentment that they felt at the fact that their ancestors had been sold into slavery by fellow Africans and not captured by the White Man. James understood but could not accept the school of thought that said, "I'm glad my ancestor didn't miss the boat when the slave ship left Africa for America!" In one poem, he described the broken shackles that occupy a ceremonial place in a coastal town. The town's chief was repulsed at the sight of human beings in bondage. He freed slaves being held for shipment and declared an end to the slave trade in his community.

The next day, George spoke of the Afros again.

"Don't forget Kennedy," he said. "Nkrumah was the first head of state to visit Kennedy at the White House. JFK was smart enough not to be worried by Nkrumah's politics. Other Americans and Europeans felt threatened by his friendship with other Third World leaders and his involvement in the Non-Aligned Movement, but Kennedy didn't. Sure, he had to placate the European allies, but he was against colonialism and he wasn't offended when Nkrumah talked about revolution and African unity. When he created the Peace Corps, Ghana was the first country to welcome Volunteers. Kennedy started other aid to Ghana, too--medical, agricultural, many things--and those things brought Afros to Ghana, too. That was the second wave of Afros who came here--the aid workers and technical people that Kennedy sent. Most of their kids went to secondary school out at Achimota, along with the children of Ghana's best families. And speak of the devil!"

George and Lucinda rose to embrace an attractive African-American professional woman in her thirties. A graduate of the "second wave," she had become a public health specialist working with an international organization in Africa. During the remainder of Promise and Wanda's stay, the parade of Afros through George and Lucinda's courtyard never ceased. The owner of the mechanics shop, the missionaries, more aid workers, the artist and craftsman--all of them seemed to exist in the orbit around "Chicken George's Afro-American Restaurant."

"Who is Osibisa?" Wanda asked. It was Sunday and she and Promise walked across the courtyard to the sitting area. "I've never heard of him."

"Oh, my Sister!" Promise exclaimed. "Where have you been? Osibisa isn't a person, it's a group. They're Ghanaian musicians who play a kind of mixture of African and African-American music. They were very popular in the 70s and had some hits in the States, just like Manu Dibango. My Mom and Dad had all their albums."

"Ahhh, Manu Dibango. At least I've heard of him," said Wanda.

"Maybe it's just a rumor, but someone said that they're playing at one of the theaters," said Promise as they sat down on a couch. "If not, let's see what movies are playing. I feel well enough to go somewhere other than the Medical Office!"

Wanda joined her on the couch. They picked up a copy of one of Ghana's tabloid newspapers that was on the coffee table and opened it to the back pages where there were adverts and announcements.

"Look, it's the picture on the wall," Promise whispered.

They both stared at the black-bordered announcement entitled, "Memorial." It contained the picture of the young army officer that was hanging on the wall of George and Lucinda's living room. The text below it memorialized the death of the young man, their son, twenty-five years earlier and invited friends and family to a church service in remembrance of him.

"It was such a stupid death."

Promise and Wanda were startled and turned to see James standing near them. He was not dressed in his usual farming clothes but in a white shirt, khaki slacks, and black shoes.

"Not many violent deaths make sense, but his was particularly senseless," James continued as he sat down on the couch across from the two young women. "Kwame worshiped Nkrumah--just like his parents, just like all of us did. Nkrumah had his faults, his excesses, and he made many mistakes, but-- George is right--he was a great man."

James looked at the paper, sighed, and continued.

"A few months after Nkrumah was overthrown, Kwame was caught up in an attempted coup. What made it stupid was that the coup leaders convinced Kwame and some other junior officers that their purpose was to re-instate Nkrumah. But that was a lie! They really just wanted to seize power for themselves! The only way that they could get anyone to follow them was to lie to them. Kwame was the only one of the plotters to be killed, and George and Lucinda and Kwame's wife never learned if he died fighting or was captured and executed."

Promise and Wanda were quiet for a moment, and then Wanda spoke.

"You and the other Afros must really love Africa," she said.

"Love Africa?" he said with a smile. "I don't know. There are times when I hate Africa as much as I love it. But like all the others--each in his own way--I live Africa, and it lives in me."

"Life goes on," said James as he rose to his feet. He nodded to the handsome young military officer who was helping his grandparents, George and Lucinda, out of their car in the driveway. His posture was ramrod straight, as befits a graduate of Sandhurst, Britain's military academy.

"He never really knew his father, but he's just like him."

THE SHRINE

"Why do we have to come here?" Ola complained. He swatted flies and wiped sweat from his brow as he and his father hiked the rain-slickened path up the side of the mountain. "We're not going to meet any of our people at the shrine. There's no one who lives there. Can't we just pay people to go up and clean out the place every once in a while? They could even make the sacrifice for us."

Ola's father, Lamassi, was so irritated at his son's whining and complaining that he stopped and snapped back at him.

"Make the sacrifice for us? You can't be serious! Do you really think that our African ancestors will receive our sacrifice well if we send someone else to do it?" he said. "Besides, what do you care? After the ceremony, we eat the chicken, don't we? You've become soft. Don't be so lazy. One of these days, when I'm too old to make this climb, it will be your job."

"Perhaps, by that time, they will have made a road up this mountain!" Ola replied. "Besides, I may not even be in the country every year when it's time for the ceremony. Wouldn't it make more sense to give the responsibility to someone else in the family, someone who's a farmer or a shopkeeper and who stays close to home?"

Lamassi was exasperated. He turned and continued his way up the path. Then, he stopped abruptly and faced Ola.

"What do you mean--'may not even be in the country every year?'" he asked. "Even if your bastard of a Director punishes you by transferring you to a remote post, you will still be in the country, still working for the Rural Development Service, and still have your rights as a civil servant to have vacation leave every year. You're just trying to make excuses to avoid fulfilling your family obligations!"

He wheeled around and resumed his trek up the hill with renewed vigor. Ola remained silent and followed.

"He's going to deal with what I said," Ola thought, "by not dealing with it. I told him that I was going to resign from the civil service and to accept a job with an international NGO in Burkina Faso. But, he's just going to ignore what I said, like it never happened."

Ola had shocked his father to the core when he announced that he intended to resign from the civil service. Lamassi did not begrudge his son the anger and frustration that he felt at the unfair and humiliating treatment by his superior in the Rural Development Service. In Lamassi's thirty years as a civil servant, he had heard such things from colleagues who felt that they were wronged. In fact, he had said them himself in moments of anger at particularly arbitrary and egregious acts by his bosses. But he and his colleagues had always thought better of their threats and found a way to soldier on. Resign from the civil service? Who would ever think seriously of such a thing? Entry into the civil service was what everyone who went to school aspired to and what every family counted on. Even a mediocre post was a guarantee of security and an opportunity for other members of one's family to obtain their education and to become civil servants themselves. Resign? It was simply ... not done!

Times are changing, he had to admit, even in the never-changing civil service. Lamassi had expected to remain a civil servant until the mandatory retirement age of 55 years. The growing numbers of educated young people, however, were pressing the government to find jobs for them, just as it had done for previous generations. No government can ignore a politically volatile generation of educated but unemployed young people. The government was finding it increasingly difficult to fulfill those expectations. It resorted to a number of devices to buy some time while it figured out how to create new jobs. It caught Lamassi by surprise when, at age 50, the government announced that all civil servants who had at least 30 years of service or who had reached the age of 50 would be retired immediately. He left the bureaucracy with mixed emotions. The brusque departure was a shock, both financially and psychologically, but if it made way for young men like his son to enter, so be it. But today, there was much to consider.

It was a long and arduous hike to get to the shrine of their ancestors. A mini-bus carried them north from their home town of Atakpamé to the town of Adjengré. They boarded a market lorry that took them west to the end of the road at the village of Fazao. From there, they continued west on foot, accompanied by three men from Fazao whom Lamassi hired every year to guide and help them. Fazao was entirely surrounded by the national park and game reserve that covers much of the central portion of the mountain range that slices from northeast to southwest down the slim length of Togo. It required a special dispensation from the Forest Service to undertake this mission every year. Normally, no one was allowed into the park on foot. It was too dangerous. The guides took foreign tourists from Fazao's lodge into the park to observe the animals safely from the vantage point of a four-wheel drive vehicle. There were elephants--at least one herd--that used to migrate back and forth to Ghana but now seemed to find it safer to stay. There were many varieties of antelope and several herds of Africa's most dangerous animal, the Cape Buffalo. There was talk of lions and leopards, but he had never seen them nor even heard their growls. There were red and gray monkeys, large troops of baboons, and occasional sightings of chimpanzees that were commonly referred to as gorillas. Lamassi had seen them all and knew how to avoid them and continue on his way.

The hiking and climbing and the necessary vigilance for wild animals distracted Lamassi's attention from this family crisis. He took caring for the shrine seriously and wanted his eldest son to do so, too.

"Instead of thinking about yourself," Lamassi said to his son, "think about the journey of our ancestors. Without their sacrifice and their hard work, where would we be?"

"Look back to the east," he continued as he turned around and pointed to the horizon behind them. "We are hundreds of kilometers from Ifè in Nigeria where our ancestors came from. Even up here on the mountain, we cannot see that far. Perhaps, on a clear day, we might see Kambolé, near our border with Bénin, where some of our people decided to stop and stay. It, too, is far. Who knows exactly why we had to leave Ifè? Certainly some of our own people must have chased us away. What was our offense? I don't know. And as our people migrated, they were threatened by the slave raiders of the Abomey Kingdom. Some of our brothers and sisters were able to stay and prosper in Kambolé, because they asked for the protection of the powerful Borgou Kingdom of the Bariba people. They paid tribute to them, and in return, the Bariba with their horsemen protected them from the Abomey raiders."

Ola had probably heard this story before but had not paid attention to it. Now, for some reason, walking in the footsteps of the ancestors, it piqued his curiosity.

"I understand that our ancestors left Ifè and went west to Kambolé and then the ones who didn't stay there continued farther west to this place of the shrine. But no one stayed here. How did it come to pass that they turned south to Atakpamé where we have been living?" Ola asked.

"They must have decided that it wasn't safe here," Lamassi replied. "To the west and southwest, they were facing the Ashanti Kingdom, who raided all the way here to capture slaves to sell to the White Man. To the northwest, they faced the Dagomba Kingdom, whose slave-raiders came on horseback. I don't think that our ancestors even stayed one generation here."

"The only ones who stayed are the ones who died and are buried here," Lamassi continued. "Our cousins in Kambolé--they take care of their obligations to our ancestors. But what of our ancestors who continued on to the place of the shrine? They gave us life and yet there is no one here to take care of them and to express to them the respect and the gratitude that they deserve. That is our responsibility, and we should fulfill that responsibility with joy and with gratitude, not with complaining."

"I apologize, Father," said Ola.

After traversing a valley between ridges, they reached the ridge of the second, higher range of mountains. Instead of continuing westward by descending onto the plains that stretched out before them below, they turned south-west and followed the ridge of the mountain for several kilometers.

"Good afternoon!"

The greeting in English of the Ghanaian Border Guard who stepped out from the shade of a tree startled Ola but not his father. Lamassi knew that they had already crossed the border into Ghana where the Ifè shrine was located.

"How are you, old friend?" he asked as they shook hands. "Ah, you have a new colleague."

The second border guard, a much younger man, came forward and joined the greetings.

"And you're still here. Still banished to this bush place in the middle of nowhere. What did you do to deserve such treatment, sleep with your superior officer's wife?" asked Lamassi, repeating the same joke that he used every year.

"My friend, you know that I like it here," the Border Guard replied. "I have my small farm with plenty to eat. I can shoot all the bush meat that I need, as long as I don't shoot in the park. There's very little to spend money on in this place, so I can save some of my salary. It is quiet and there is very little traffic through here and so I look forward to your yearly visits. You're very generous, too, and for that I am grateful."

Lamassi's generosity was well-founded. It required the services of one of the porters to carry all the liquor and rice and canned goods that he brought for the Border Guards but it assured good will. Even when Ghana and Togo had a political spat and the border was ostensibly closed for 18 months, Lamassi made his annual visits to the shrine and crossed this remote border point without incident. There was little chance that the shrine would be disturbed, but the Guards on their patrols would notice if anything was out of order and send off a message to him.

The Guards accompanied the pilgrims down the path to the shrine.

Ola did not know what he had been expecting but the shrine was certainly not impressive. It measured no more than six or seven meters square. The walls were made of gray stones that had obviously been gathered near at hand. The stone masonry was done well enough. The mud mortar that held the stones together was protected from erosion by a layer of cement plaster that was slathered into the gaps between the stones. The roof was made of tin sheets nailed on teak pole rafters and the door and windows were made of wood frames covered with tin sheets. While his first impression was not a positive one, Ola had to admit upon further consideration that the stone building fit naturally into its its rocky and wooded surroundings.

There was a latch on the front door but no padlock.

"Sometimes we take cover from the rain here," said the Border Guard, "when we're out on patrol in the rainy season."

"We need to clean the place out," said Lamassi. "But first, let's see what animals we must rout from the place. In past years, we've found birds and bats, we've found snakes--a boa, a viper--so let's be careful and sweep the place clean."

Everyone in the group entered with ease and set about their habitual tasks. Since Ola was new to the shrine, he was the last to enter. He moved forward gingerly and allowed his eyes to adjust to the dark of the shelter. He started when he saw what he thought was a man crouched down on the floor in the center of the room, but he quickly recognized it as an earthen statue. He had never seen one exactly like it before, but he recognized the shape of the head as typical of the representations made by his Ifè people and their Yoruba cousins from Nigeria. It was covered in faded paints in various colors. Chicken feathers from previous sacrifices were stuck in dried blood on the statue's head.

Before long, the pounded earth floor of the shrine was swept clean. They were fortunate. The only beasts that inhabited the place this time were spiders and a scorpion. It was nearing dusk, and the pilgrims laid out the woven straw mats that they carried with them. They stepped outside and quickly found firewood for a cooking fire set up between three rocks that could support cooking pans. Even though it had been raining, they found sufficient dry kindling inside the shrine. Before long, they had a fire underway and the humid wood produced a heavy smoke and spit and popped as the fire dried the wood.

They were hungry, but they had little strength left for cooking. Sandwiches of sardines and oil in split French bread *baguettes* had sufficed during the climb. The fire allowed them to boil water for tea and to heat the canned mackerel in tomato sauce that they spread over *gari*, the starchy meal made from grated and dried cassava. *Gari* would be the breakfast that accompanied their morning coffee, too. Thick syrupy sweetened condensed milk made *gari* a perfectly adequate breakfast cereal and it also diluted the bitterness of the "Made in Côte d'Ivoire" Nescafé that they had carried with them in small tins. Hard remnants of the previous day's *baguettes* became edible when dipped in the *café au lait*.

The shrine's shelter was not comfortable but at least it was dry. Remnants of plastic bags slid underneath the straw mats to block whatever dampness rose through the floor. The *pagnes*--two-meter lengths of cloth--and their plastic rain ponchos helped to keep in their body warmth and ward off the cool dampness in the air.

"Our ancestors chose well to pick this place," said Ola the next morning as he bent over the stream of cold water that bubbled out of the side of the slope and continued down the hill, where it joined other rivulets along the away to form a stream. He used a gourd to wet himself with the icy cold water and then to rinse off the soap.

"Look," he continued. "There is water here in abundance. From this vantage point, you can look out over the plains to the west and see any enemies before they see you. The plains at the foot of the mountain look lush. I am sure that they made good farms for our people. Down in the morning and back up the mountain at night. I would think that they were safe here."

"Safe, to a point, I suppose," replied his father as he, too, accomplished his morning *toilettes,* "but our people were not numerous. And they were not warlike. Remember, we Yoruba peoples--whether we're Ifè or Oyo or whatever--we are "Africa's botanists" and its artists and musicians and intellectuals. Oh, there were mighty Yoruba kingdoms in Nigeria, no doubt about it, but war is not what we are mainly known for. And war is what our ancestors must have been fleeing when they left Ifè."

"It must have been disappointing to have to pick up and leave again," said Ola, "and to leave behind the graves of family members."

"They were threatened by mighty forces that were well armed and on horseback. They must have thought it wiser to continue south," explained Lamassi. "After a generation or two of moving and trying to find a safe place to live, I'm sure that they were happy to settle down when they arrived at our present home. But even at our present home, these Abomey people came and attacked us more than once!"

It was time to begin the ceremonies. Lamassi carried the large white rooster that he had procured for the occasion. One of the porters had carried it in one of the baskets that are specifically woven as cages for transporting fowl. Shaped like an onion, the point was attached to a rope that could be tied to a pole that was suspended across the shoulders of two porters if that was necessary. A small woven flap was tied shut over the opening and the woven matting was open enough to allow sufficient air for breathing.

Ola trailed behind and watched. There were two poles of interest for the ceremony: the statue inside the shrine and the area where the graves of the ancestors, unmarked and obscured by weather and plant growth, were located. Lamassi began at the grave area where he performed several libations. He kneeled down and sipped from a gourd filled with water before pouring the drink on the ground. He repeated the gesture with a bottle filled with distilled palm wine, called *sodabi*. Gesturing first to the left, then to the right, and finally in front of him, he invoked the names of the ancestors that had been passed down from generation to generation. He begged the ancestors to accept their humble gifts and, with them, the thanks of their descendants for giving them life. He implored them to continue to watch over their descendants and, on their behalf, to intervene with God and the spirits of nature for mercy and for the protection of their children.

The libations were simple and brief. The party retreated to the shrine. They entered the shelter and stood before the adobe statue with its familiar round features. Lamassi took the white rooster from one of the porters and a sharp knife from another. He extended the rooster out over the statue and slit its throat half-way through. He allowed its blood to spill out and pour over the head of its statue, all the while uttering incantations to the deity represented by the statue. He implored it to continue to be an ever-watchful sentinel and to guard the path leading to the resting place of the ancestors and to protect and preserve their peaceful repose. Finally he backed away from the statue, knelt down, and dropped the rooster at the base of the statue. He stood and stepped back again. Together, the group watched the macabre dance of the dying fowl as it scurried and floundered around the room for many minutes before finally coming to rest near the statue.

"Aha!" said Lamassi with a satisfied smile on his face. "Our offering has been accepted."

"Did you see how long he struggled before dying?" Lamassi asked Ola. "That's a good omen. If he had simply gone limp and died, it would mean that our offering was inadequate and unacceptable."

Lamassi and the porters moved quickly to pluck and butcher the rooster, stopping only momentarily to smear feathers into the blood that covered the statue's head. Before long, it was being grilled over a fire.

"Is that all there is?" asked Ola.

"What did you expect?" replied his father. "Thunder and lightning? Apparitions? Voices?"

"I suppose so," admitted his son with a sheepish smile.

"We have come to visit and honor our ancestors," Lamassi explained. "We thanked them and asked them to continue to watch over and protect us. And we begged the divinity to secure our ancestors' resting place and our request was well-received. Now, it's over. It's done. We'll eat the rooster, just like I promised. And we'll come back next year and do the same thing over again."

The prospect of coming back next year and doing the same thing over again was both boring and annoying to Ola before they embarked on this trip. Yet, simple as they were, the ceremonies had moved Ola in ways that he never expected. Or, more precisely, he was moved by both the ceremonies and by the trek. He had not thought much about his ethnic group, his Ifè people, in spite of the fact that, small as it was, it had given Togo one of its Presidents and was not insignificant in the life of his small country. For many years, he had studied and worked in places where he had little occasion to speak his mother tongue and was more likely to speak French and Éwé than Ifè in his daily life. The effort that the trek required had somehow made Ola begin to feel a quiet pride in his people and their history and culture that was entirely unexpected.

It did not take long to dispense with the rooster. Even though there was only one, it was a large bird and everyone partook.

"Thanks once again to the Americans for filling a poor African man's belly," said Lamassi to the delight of his companions. The rooster was one of a breed introduced from America to provide for meatier birds. "There was no handshake label on him, but we appreciate him all the same!"

The trek back to Fazao was mainly downhill and went briskly with little talk along the way.

In the back of a pick-up taxi from Fazao back to the main North-South highway, Ola began to speak of the trek.

"Father, thank you for insisting that I accompany you," said Ola. "I didn't want to come but I'm glad I did. Somehow, I feel closer to our people now. I even feel like I know something more about myself."

Lamassi was silent for a while before speaking.

"There is much to learn from the struggles of our ancestors," he said. "When they were threatened, they set out upon a long voyage. Fleeing from brothers who had become enemies, they were threatened by the slave raiders wherever they went. They thought that they had found a new home on this mountain and began to settle in. But they had to adjust and change when they were faced with a new threat. And so they did what was necessary to do to survive and to find a safe home for their families and for our people. When we are confronted by a threat, by a challenge, sometimes we must muster the courage to make a change--to set out upon a voyage in a new direction to find safer and happier surroundings."

Lamassi was silent again. As they approached the highway where they would change to a bus back home, he spoke.

"They say," said Lamassi, "that Bobo Dioulasso is a nice town. It's the old colonial capital of Burkina Faso, with wide streets planted with trees."

He paused.

"Will your new employers grant you leave next year when it is time to do the ceremony?" he asked.

"As long as I ask for it well in advance, I'm sure that they will grant it,"

Ola replied with a smile.

As the bush taxi pulled into the taxi station at the main highway, the mini-bus to Atakpamé came in view and Lamassi spoke.

"Let's go home."

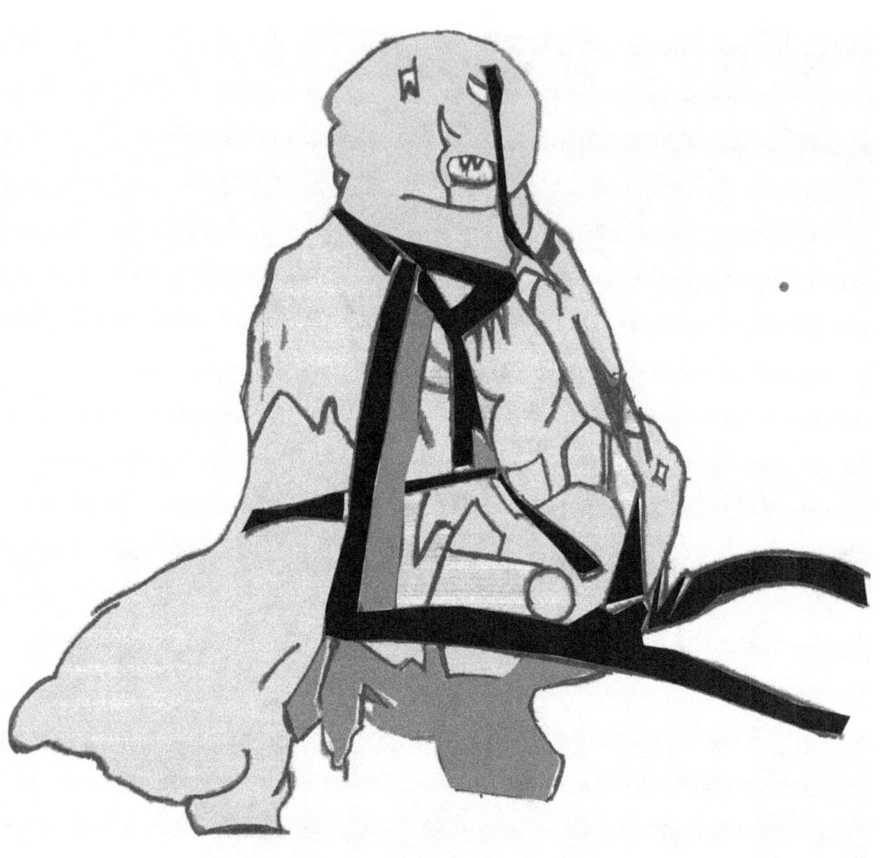

ATOMIC JUNCTION

Lilabatoma was a young Losso man from the Kara Region of Northern Togo. He came to settle down far from his home in a small town in my country, Ghana. Atomic Junction is not really a town. You won't find it on any map. It is just a crossroad where homes and businesses and a market have grown up around a petrol station and a lorry park, but I can tell you how it came to be called Atomic Junction. It's all because of our first President of Ghana, Kwame Nkrumah.

Nkrumah built a super-highway from Accra, our capital city, to Tema, our largest port city. It began at the roundabout called Tetteh Quarshie Circle. It was a straight, beautiful divided highway with concrete lanes on each side of wide green parkways, just like in America.

At the roundabout, however, if you passed up the highway to Tema and turned north, you passed through the small towns that had become Accra's suburbs. After a few miles, you came to a crossroad where a faded sign read, "Ghana Atomic Energy Commission," with an arrow pointing to the west.

We gained our independence during the "Atomic Age" and Nkrumah meant for our country to participate in it, just like the Europeans. The GAEC is still there, but we have no nuclear power plants, no atomic bombs. "Atomic Junction" is what we call our crossroad community and it is thriving just the same.

There were many Lossos living in Accra and in the plantations. They were very hardworking and honest people and we liked having them in our country. They came from a very poor area and were willing to do the jobs that we Ghanaians did not like to do. They manned the sanitation trucks collecting human waste at night. They dug graves. They were porters in markets. They did the most backbreaking work on construction sites. They wielded cutlasses well, keeping the plantations clean and harvesting coffee and cocoa. They also served loyally in our army and police force.

Normally, we would have baptized Lilabatoma with an Akan day-name and the name of his ethnic group. There were many Kwassi Lossos and Kwame Kotokolis and Kofi Kabrays. As Ghana passed through periods of hard times, however, such names made it easier to identify a foreigner who was allegedly taking a job or a business opportunity from a "true Ghanaian." Many of Lilabatoma's countrymen were changing their names, even taking Muslim names because a Muslim name could as easily be Ghanaian as not. In his case, however, he already had a shortened name.

"Just call me Toma," he said, and the nickname stuck.

Toma was a "drivers mate," an apprentice to Awassé, a man from his home region who owned and drove a lorry for long-distance transport. Toma received no wages. In fact, his family had to pay Awassé so that he would take him for a four-year apprenticeship and teach him how to be a driver. Awassé gave him only shelter and food. In the early years of his apprenticeship, Toma had learned little about actual driving. He and his fellow apprentices were free labor for the most onerous and menial tasks. They had to wash the lorry and help keep it repaired and in good condition. At every stop, they helped load and unload passengers and cargo and squeezed the maximum of both into the lorry. Finally, when it was time to roll they had to push the old lorry to start it and to pick up the bulky wooden wedges that were placed behind the wheels to keep the lorry from rolling. They threw the wedges into the back of the lorry and leaped onto the tailgate as it picked up speed and drove away.

Awassé's vehicle was an old Bedford seven-ton lorry. He had removed the steel bed and replaced it with a sturdy wooden box structure. On the first level, passengers sat on hard wooden benches and, wherever there were no passengers, cargo such as sacks of grain or bags of cement filled all available space. Then, they put thick wooden poles to span the space between the outside walls and above the heads of the passengers to form a "second story." There, they stacked the passengers' bags and the rest of the cargo. When it reached the point where the lorry might be in risk of tipping over, they stopped and covered it all with a tarp that they tied down with a crisscrossing web of ropes. Atop all this was where Toma and the other apprentices rode, exposed to the elements--heat, wind, rain, thunder, and lightning as well as dust and dirt. They kept the tarp strapped down, repaired any broken or frayed ropes, and re-arranged any baggage or cargo that had shifted.

Any stragglers among the passengers for whom there was no room inside also had to mount on top with the apprentices. Those who were smart heeded the tales that were passed around the transport community. They looped their belts through the ropes that were holding down the tarpaulin.

"If you don't tie yourself," the older boys told Toma, "a bump in the road or even a small accident will throw you to a certain death."

Like all lorries and the smaller "Mammy Wagons," Awassé's lorry sported a colorfully painted motto. In pidgin English, "How for do?" meant, "What can one do?" and indicated the determination and the resignation with which one must go forward in life.

Toma looked at the motto and took it to heart.

"To be a driver's mate is hard, oh! It is very hard," he reported to his family. "I must sacrifice now to prepare for my future. When I finish my apprenticeship, I will find a job as a driver. One day, I will own my own lorry--I swear that I will!"

Toma frequently traveled through "Atomic Junction." Awassé plied the less frequent route between their home in the Kara Region of Northern Togo and Accra. Most transporters left Accra and followed the coastal road to Lomé, the capital of Togo. From there, they took the National Road Number One from Lomé northward to the Kara Region and retraced their steps in returning to Accra. Awassé traveled from Nima, the Accra slum, in a northeasterly direction passing through Atomic Junction and through the Eastern Region to cross the Volta River at the Akossombo Dam. He continued north through Ghana's Volta Region and crossed over the border when he neared the Togolese towns of Kpalimé or Badou. Sometimes he ventured more than 400 kilometers from the coast before crossing near the Togolese town of Bassar.

This itinerary served the people from their home region who lived in Accra. It also linked the home region directly to the coffee- and cocoa-growing areas in the Volta Region where many of their people worked as sharecroppers. This route and the side roads and paths that Awassé often took had fewer police and customs barricades and therefore fewer bribes to be paid.

You wouldn't know it to look at him, but Awassé had been a politician in the days before and immediately following Togo's Independence. He was a big fish in the small pond that was his home region. A token northerner in the political party of Togo's first President, he had even been part of a parliamentary delegation that traveled to the United States and met with President John F. Kennedy. It was not long, however, before the President abolished opposition political parties and drove the opposition's leaders into jail or into exile. Friends in Lomé warned Awassé of the regime's excesses and alerted him to impending trouble. The warnings came just in time for him to quit in protest and to avoid being taken down in the military coup d'état on January 13, 1963.

In his home region, those who had suffered under the old regime and those whom Awassé had treated with arrogance and disrespect resented him. He had been a self-important political operative who could not be approached directly--you had to see an intermediary first. He was smart enough, however, to abandon politics after the coup and to concentrate on his transport business and other commercial activities.

His lorry was an old and ramshackle one, a description that fit Awassé as well. He was short and thick. He was always unkempt and smeared with motor oil. His clothes smelled of the homemade diesel fuel that he concocted from mixing kerosene and motor oil in order to save money. His breath betrayed the strong odor of *apateshie*, the local "African gin" that he favored, and his eyes were perpetually bloodshot and yellow.

Awassé's morning began early. He stumbled into the corner bar at the crack of dawn and cried out his order.

"Kerosene!" he yelled. "Give me some kerosene, barman, so that I can light my lamp."

The barman placed the first of several shot glasses before him.

Apateshie was theoretically illegal. That is why they called it "kerosene" with a wink of the eye. The bar owner made it at a still hidden in the bush.

The real liquor was made by felling oil nut palm trees, extracting the palm wine, and then distilling it. There were fewer palm trees these days, so the barman would distill anything--corn, sugar cane, or anything that would ferment. He added herbs that gave the drink a rusty red-brown appearance.

"Still making it from rusty nails and old carburetors, eh?" Awassé said as he contemplated the bottle.

The barman rarely replied. He was quiet and sober and kept close track of his business.

"My business is making money, not making *apateshie*," he told his closest friends. "If I could profit more by selling something else, I would stop selling *apateshie* right away."

On the road, Awassé struggled with the steering wheel of his lorry as if he were wrestling with a gorilla from the bush. There was so much "play" in it that it required spinning the wheel in an exaggerated fashion in order to effect a maneuver, let alone a turn. The state of the transmission and clutch was always suspect. As Awassé drove, Toma or one of his mates had to ride herd on the gear shift lever to keep it from popping out of gear. It was so frightening for the young driver's mates that they felt safer crawling around on top of the baggage while careening down the road than being in the cabin with Awassé.

Toma liked to stop at Atomic Junction. In his brief but frequent forays into the market during their stops, Toma had made the acquaintance of a young woman who was a hawker. Mina carried on her head a tray containing empty sardine and tomato paste tins full of roasted groundnuts for sale. She was a voluptuous young woman who preferred to walk barefoot and favored tight-fitting dresses and bright colored brassieres from the used clothing market. Her mother had a small kiosk near the lorry park where she sold cigarettes and all manner of small items as well as plastic bags of ice water that she kept in an insulated cooler.

One day when they stopped at Atomic Junction, Toma had Mina on his mind more than Awassé's work. Toma was flirting with Mina when Awassé got into the cab of his lorry, sounded his horn, and called to his apprentices. As was the young macho apprentice routine, Toma feigned not to notice that the lorry was pulling away, and then tried to impress Mina and the crowd by sprinting off, gathering the wedges, and leaping onto the back of the lorry just at the last moment as it was gaining speed. This time, however, he miscalculated. He threw the wedges into the back but missed his leap onto the lorry and fell to the road. To Toma's amazement, Awassé continued to drive away, leaving him behind in the cloud of red clay dust and diesel fumes that the lorry stirred up in its wake. His mates scrambled toward the front of the lorry and yelled to Awassé. They waved to Toma, mocking him at first but encouraging him to keep running.

"*O dey go*! *O dey go*!" they screamed at him. "*Kabba-kabba-lo*! Hurry!"

Finally, they realized that Awassé had no intention of stopping. The lorry disappeared from sight. On board was the little money that Toma had, his few belongings, and his Togolese National Identity Card.

Toma waited patiently at the lorry park for Awassé to return and pick him up as he was sure he would do. Awassé would be very angry if he returned to Atomic Junction and then had to continue all the way back to Accra to find Toma. For several hours he followed Mina around the market as she sold groundnuts. Eventually, he understood that, if Awassé was going to return for him, it would not be on this day. He had no money, no food, and no shelter. A muscular young man, Toma quickly found small jobs to earn some subsistence money. He pushed lorries, carried bags of grain, and pulled carts of merchandise for tips. He earned enough to fill his belly and spent the night on the hard concrete floor of one of our market stalls.

Little did he know that the political and personal enmity between the Presidents of our two countries would boil over soon thereafter. By the time that Awassé arrived in his home region, word came that the Ghana-Togo border was closed.

Back in Atomic Junction, Toma found that it was easy to keep busy if you were willing to work hard. He had no trouble finding small-small jobs in the market. More and more people saw that he was reliable and energetic. Hours turned into days and days turned into weeks as he waited for the border to reopen. As busy as he was, he still found time to flirt with Mina. While she appreciated the attention, she became increasingly frustrated that Toma had not moved beyond flirtation. One day, she unexpectedly lashed out at him in the middle of the marketplace.

"Every day, every day," she taunted him, "you stop here. You come to market to bother me when I should be selling. Even ground-nuts, if I don' sell, I don' chop, ohhh. Talk-talk is all you do. Why you no do not'ing? Why you no touch me? You got no *bangala*? You leave it for lorry, dey take 'am back for Togo?"

All at once, Mina's expression turned from mocking and contemptuous to surprise, and finally to sympathy.

"Oh, I sorry," she said. "Man come and thief your *bangala*! So sorry."

Mina had heard the rumors that were rampant in the country. According to hysterical reports on the radio and in the tabloid newspapers, some people were stealing the male organs of unsuspecting men, and occasionally the breasts of unsuspecting women, in broad daylight. These evil people accomplished their devilish deeds through magic simply by touching a person on the shoulder. In one town after another, the accused witches were immediately set upon by angry crowds. If they were lucky, the police or some Good Samaritan spirited them away. Those who were not so fortunate were lynched.

"Is true," she continued. "You dey go and lost your *bangala*!"

"No be so!" Toma replied indignantly.

"Eef 'e no be so," she inquired "why you no go touch me?"

Mina issued a challenge to Toma. Her mother was traveling and her kiosk was closed. They would step inside the kiosk and he would prove his manhood. He would prove that he still had his *bangala*. At first, Toma was embarrassed and refused. Mina continued to taunt him, to the great amusement of everyone in the market.

Finally, Toma relented. He grabbed Mina by her arm and dragged her to her mother's kiosk. She unlocked it and they went inside and closed the door behind them as a crowd of spectators gathered. It was not long before the small kiosk began rocking on its foundations accompanied by sounds like animals from the forest. After a while, it became quiet and Toma and Mina came out, blinking their eyes in the bright sunlight. Toma had an ear-to-ear grin on his face. Mina reattached her cloth and smoothed it with her hands.

"I am satisfied," she announced in a matter-of-fact way. She replaced the tray of groundnuts on her head and walked away.

The crowd signaled its approval. Men slapped Toma on his back.

With the border sealed, lorries going to Togo had to travel all the way north to Bawku in the extreme northeast corner of Ghana. They would have to cross the border into Burkina Faso and then turn south to cross the Togo border. From there, their voyage would take them an additional 200 kilometers back southward to the Kara Region. The border closing meant that the length of their route would be nearly doubled. It would cost more fuel, more wear-and-tear on the lorry, and more bribes. It was no longer worth the trip except in the most extreme circumstances. Travel and commerce effectively stopped. The border had been closed before, but this time it remained closed for the next 18 months.

It was nearly two years after his last voyage when Awassé finally returned from Togo for the first time. He stopped in Atomic Junction on his way to Accra and inquired at the petrol station as to what had become of his former apprentice.

"Where is that fool of an apprentice that I left behind?" he asked the owner of the petrol station. "I brought his Togolese national identity card. They say he has stayed here all this time. I always told my apprentices that if they ever missed getting on the lorry, they should just stay and wait. I never imagined that he would be stupid enough to wait for two years!"

"Apprentice? What apprentice?" was the response. "Ah, you mean Toma?"

By that time, most of us didn't even remember that his name was Toma.

After the challenge, Mina's mother had returned from traveling to find her daughter pregnant. Toma did not shirk his responsibilities. He moved into his new mother-in-law's house. He proved that he was not only a hard worker but also that he was willing to do anything to support his small family that grew to include a baby daughter. He was a porter, a lorry-pusher, and a book-man, finding and booking passengers and cargo for the transporters.

Eventually, Toma became a *susu* man. He collected and safeguarded the market sellers' modest daily savings in exchange for a small monthly fee and for the right to make short-term investments with the money. He would go through the market at the end of each day to make his collections.

"Yes-yes! Yes-yes!" he called out to alert the women to prepare their deposits.

He proved to be impeccably honest. He never failed to return a woman's savings to her at the appointed date. At the same time, his own income grew steadily.

As the months passed, Toma improved his command of our languages, Ga and Twi, and he demonstrated unexpected qualities of character. His smile was constant but sincere. He was a neutral third party. We came to trust him for his sense of fairness and his conciliatory nature. We called upon him to mediate disputes and to help keep order. Even the police decided to ignore his lack of identity papers because he was a valuable member of the community and they came to rely upon him, too.

That's why we call him "The Mayor." It may not be official, but for us, he is the indispensable "Mayor of Atomic Junction!"

LOS TUPAMAROS RENDEZ-VOUS BAR

"Los Tupamaros--dey be tuff, ohhh!" said Thankful.

Several of her friends and I were sitting around a table with Thankful in her establishment--"Los Tupamaros Rendez-Vous Bar." It was situated on the first floor of a large two-story block building on a dirt road near the Main Post Office in Togo's capital city, Lomé. She was speaking "pidgin English," but Thankful was an intelligent woman and she was not uneducated. An Anlo-Éwé from Keta on Ghana's southeastern coast near the border and Togo's capital city, Lomé, she had received a primary school education near her home.

Thankful alternated between proper English, pidgin, and Éwé in her conversation. I was pleased that she often chose to speak pidgin or Éwé to me, rather than the "White Man's Language." She kept the bar's accounts in a schoolchild's copy book. They were simple but complete and well-maintained. She showed them to me and I could not improve upon them.

On that day, I had gently initiated a conversation about the origins of her bar's name. It was stupid of me, however, to presume to enlighten her about the true identity of "Los Tupamaros." They were the so-called "prototypical Latin American urban guerrillas" who wreaked havoc in Uruguay in the 1960s and 1970s. Political consciousness-raising was not the order of the day and I retreated quickly.

"Yes," I agreed with a sigh. "They are definitely very, very tough people."

"Ahhhh, you see!" said Thankful with satisfaction as she punched her friend Fati on the shoulder. "Dey be tuff, oh! Is good."

Thankful's home town, Keta, was once an important port for the slave trade. After the end of slavery, the town slowly but inevitably deteriorated. The construction of the Akossombo Dam that created "Man's Greatest Lake" on the mighty Volta River had a powerful effect on the estuary. It caused the inexorable beach erosion that cut off the coastal road between Ghana's capital city, Accra, and Lomé. In Keta itself, many streets, stores, schools, churches, and homes were wiped away. Commerce moved to Lomé and beyond and took the people with it. Thankful and her extended family that counted in its midst many shrewd businesswomen moved, too.

"Los Tupamaros" was centrally located not only near to the post office but also near to other government offices, to stores, and to the city's central market. It was on a corner and was well situated to keep the bar full of regulars and passers-by alike. In addition to beer, Thankful bought large glass demi-johns of Algerian wine--popularly know as "headaches-in-a-bottle"--and poured it into empty beer bottles for individual sale. She also sold *sodabi*--African "white lightning"--by the shot. As business progressed, the establishment became as much a *maquis* as a bar, serving local cuisine at prices her clientele could afford. At the end of the day, the bar filled and it stayed loud and busy until after midnight, even on weekdays.

One evening, a young Frenchman named Marcel and his Togolese teaching colleagues came to "Los Tupamaros." A meal of pounded plantain fufu and palm soup with smoked fish and garden eggs was followed by an evening of drinking beer. Marcel's friends introduced him to the proprietor of the bar, Thankful, and the Togolese ritual flirting began with the obligatory opening line.

"Good evening, Madame," Marcel said. "It is Madame, isn't it? Or is it Mademoiselle?"

Marcel instantly fell in love with Thankful and the feeling was mutual. It was not long before they were inseparable in Lomé and pining for each other when Marcel had to return to his teaching post in the north.

Marcel was from a working-class family and had only a tenth grade diploma. He was self-conscious about the fact that he was the least educated of the young draftees who were fulfilling their military obligation with the French version of the Peace Corps. He was assigned to teach in the lower grades at a junior secondary school--grades 7 through 10--at Koussanté.

Situated 500 kilometers from the coast, Koussanté was considered an undesirable post by both Togolese and expatriates. It was hot, dry, and dusty. Not much in the way of services or supplies was available to make life more bearable. Meat was available and cheap. The stores and markets never lacked the basic necessities but never stocked luxuries. It was a place where civil servants were exiled for some real or imagined offense, such as a man sleeping with his boss's wife, or a female civil servant thwarting the advances of a male supervisor. The morale of the exiles was not high.

"Welcome to the armpit of Togo," were the first words from one of his colleagues.

"It doesn't seem so bad to me," Marcel responded evenly. "Perhaps I don't mind coming here because my expectations were not high. The place that I come from in France is not special, either."

His colleague just shook his head and walked away.

"You'll see," he said over his shoulder. "Wait till the dry season. You won't be so cheerful then!"

Koussanté worked out well for Marcel. It presented few distractions and his fellow teachers were his primary associates. Marcel dealt with the situation as an opportunity rather than a misfortune. He was respected as a teacher. At the same time, he assiduously studied for his baccalaureate diploma. During school vacations, he took advantage of courses offered at the teacher training college in order to enhance his teaching credentials. After his 18-month military obligation was finished, he prolonged his volunteer teaching service for several years. He continued to study and eventually presented himself as an independent candidate for the baccalaureate examination. He passed it and had realistic hopes of continuing his studies and obtaining a university degree.

Between Marcel's visits to Lomé, he and Thankful corresponded frequently and passionately. He repeatedly begged her to move to Koussanté to join him and to create a business there. She steadfastly refused.

Thankful only visited Koussanté once. She found it a pleasant enough town but boring. There was nothing to do there but work and study. The Atacora-Togo Mountain Range loomed majestically to the south. The wooded savanna with its plains and low rolling hills that stretched out northward was largely inhabited by the wild animals of the National Park.

Thankful enjoyed the mountain scenery and seeing the wild animals in the park but, she said, "The animals don't spend money."

"Is no business here," she told Marcel. "Better for me to stay for Lomé with the bar. If I do more--cook more food, our African chop--I can make more money. Then, I can do other businesses, too, with my mother, my aunties, and sisters. I trust them. If I try to do business here, who will work with me?"

She returned to Lomé and not long afterward found that she was pregnant. She was delighted for a child who would bind her to Marcel and him to her. In addition, every family in Togo at this time wanted at least one half-caste child. Months later, she gave birth to a baby girl who quickly became the center of attention of the extended family.

Marcel only got to spend time with Thankful and their daughter during school breaks and vacations. He still wanted for them to move to Koussanté to join him. Marcel became even more frustrated and lonely than ever.

"Me? Move to that bush place with our pikin'?" she exclaimed. "'E no possible."

From time to time, when I stopped by "Los Tupamaros," Thankful would invite me up to her room above the bar. The first time, I hesitated. Marcel was not my friend, but I lived and worked not far from Koussanté and had met him on occasion. Even though Marcel had never legally married Thankful, they had fulfilled the traditional obligations of marriage. He always referred to her as his wife and everyone addressed her as "Madame." I felt uncomfortable, but Thankful put me at ease.

"Marcel have girlfriend to play wit', up d'ere in Koussanté," she said. "So why not me, too? I am human being, just like him. I am black, he is white, but I am human being, too. So, if he can play, why I can't play?"

Thankful was well-informed. Marcel had indeed taken up with one of his colleagues at the junior secondary school of Koussanté. One of the rare female teachers at the secondary level, Solange was from a nearby village. She was the daughter of a retired non-commissioned officer who served in France's wars in Indo-China and Algeria and the younger sister of a junior officer in the Togolese Army. She was quiet, serious, and studious with enormous horn-rim glasses and a pleasant smile.

One day, I dropped by "Los Tupamaros" and once again Thankful invited me up to her room. It was obvious, however, that this time Thankful had not invited me up to her room to play. She was very sad. When we sat down on her bed she began to cry as she showed me a letter.

"Why he do dis?" she asked. "Write to my mother and say bad t'ings about me. Why?"

"If he don't want me," she continued. "Then, he make an' go. I don' keep 'am here. Even our pikin--our daughter--if he wan' her, I can't say no. But why he say dese bad t'ings?"

She handed me the letter. I opened it. It was written in English, from Marcel to Thankful's mother. In it, he accused Thankful of all manner of transgressions and offenses to him. For his part, he had only showered her with kindnesses, not the least of which was having a bright and beautiful daughter with her. He accused her of infidelities and did not refrain from labeling her a harlot. Finally, he accused her of stealing a ring from him. It was not a valuable ring in monetary terms, but it was an heirloom that had been in his family for many years and had great sentimental value to him. He pleaded with Thankful's mother to persuade her to return the ring to him.

"You see," she said. "To my mother, he accuse me of bein' harlot an' a teef, too. Accuse me to my mother. Why he did that? I no be teef! And himself is not harlot?"

"I don't know what to say, Thankful," I said. "This is awful. It's a mean thing to do. If he wanted to end things between you, he should just be man enough to say so, face-to-face. He should not have sent this to your mother. What can your mother do? What can your mother say? Why should he say such bad things about you to your mother? I don't know. This is not the way that a man should act toward a woman."

I wished that I had something helpful to say to her. I felt inadequate to the task before me. The only service that I could render was that of my physical presence and my sympathy.

It is not admirable but perhaps not totally unexpected that, as Marcel improved his own education and his own station in life, he would desire a companion whose level of education and professional status corresponded more closely to his own.

The connection between Marcel and Solange did have a certain logic to it. Marcel was not from the traditional elite of his country but he had seized upon the opportunity for education afforded by his alternative to military service as a step up to a more elevated social status and a better economic future. The home region of Solange's family was far from the coast and the coastal elite that had once bought and sold their forefathers and monopolized access to education and wealth. Her family, too, had seized upon military service as the alternative path to upward mobility and better employment opportunities through access to education.

Marcel and Thankful and the various minor players in this drama seemed to carry on their lives and loves like the characters in the soap operas that were rapidly becoming ubiquitous on African television screens. "African Wisdom," the wisdom of the ancestors, had manifested itself to me on many occasions and I was grateful for it, but it did not appear to be present this time.

The daughter that Thankful had with Marcel was a frequent presence at "Los Tupamaros" under the watchful eyes of Thankful's mother and a teenage nanny. The toddler was bright and funny and reveled in being the center of attention. She spent time with Marcel and Solange when they came down to Lomé. Inevitably, the time came for Marcel to return to France, where he planned to complete his university education. He wanted to take his daughter with him to France. He married Solange at a ceremony in Koussanté attended by many high-ranking officers of the Togolese Army. She agreed to be the stepmother of his child and to raise her with him.

According to local customary law, Thankful could have fought the change of custody, at least until the child was old enough to go to school and perhaps longer. She had the right to receive child support. Even if she gave Marcel custody, she might have blocked him from taking the child to France. Keeping custody from Marcel and preventing him from taking their daughter to France, however, would have deprived the child of her chances for a better education and of her opportunity for a better life in Europe. Thankful could only hope to try to keep a relationship with her daughter by telephone, by letter, and hopefully by visits.

"One day, when my pikin' is grow up, she go bring me, her mother, to stay with her in France."

"African Wisdom" was perhaps manifest in its most practical and pragmatic form after all.

"You have to be tough to make such a decision," I said.

"Tuff, yah," she replied with an ironic smile. "Tuff like Tupamaros."

As much as I enjoyed being invited to Thankful's room, I visited the bar less frequently when I was in town. I knew that Thankful would be missing her daughter. I still had no way of comforting her for the separation. I did not look forward to listening to her vent her anger at her mistreatment by Marcel. By the time I dropped by one day for a visit, her daughter had already been in France with Marcel and Solange for more than a year.

"I have new photos of my pikin," she announced proudly as she spread the pictures out on the table in front of me. "She's a big girl now, and smart!"

As I looked at the pictures, a strange sense of familiarity came over me, as if I had seen the photos somewhere before.

In fact, I had seen them, or rather, pictures very much like them. The pictures of Thankful's daughter looked stunningly, exactly like pictures of my mother and my sister when they were her same age. I could have been looking at my own daughter.

GILLES, THE *PETIT-BLANC*

Gilles always shows up at meal time" was the standing joke in Lomé among both his expatriate and Togolese friends and associates. Gilles was a congenial fellow and an agreeable conversationalist. Few people would turn him away from their table, as long as his visits were not daily. He was intelligent enough to spread himself around town.

"He means no harm," said a Togolese woman who was a mutual acquaintance. "Gilles is just a *petit-blanc*."

She smiled at finding the exact words to describe a phenomenon hitherto unknown in Lomé. The term, *petit-blanc*, was new to me, too. I had not yet spent much time in the larger francophone cities of West Africa--Abidjan, Dakar, and Douala--where both the phenomenon and the term were well-known. A *petit-blanc* was a low-income white person with few credentials or skills, usually a Frenchman, who had settled in an African country to seek his fortune. I had easily divined its irony. In those days, there was usually nothing *petit* about a white person in West Africa. On the contrary, a white person was usually a big man or a boss--if not in physical stature, at least in wealth, privilege, and security relative to his African neighbors.

Gilles first came to Africa from France as a military draftee fulfilling his alternative service as a volunteer in Bénin. The unsuccessful invasion of Cotonou several years earlier led by an infamous French mercenary had left the regime particularly paranoid, especially in regard to any expatriates in its midst. Nationalization of banks and enterprises and the general decline in economic activity led many European businesspeople and also many Lebanese merchants to move down the coast to Lomé, Accra, or Abidjan. Fortunes were still being made in Bénin in the local parallel economy. By the end of his eighteen-month service, Gilles knew that he had neither the cultural knowledge nor the wherewithal to play on this field. For him to strike out on his own in search of his fortune, Bénin did not offer the best opportunities. He migrated west to Lomé.

Lomé was no longer the boomtown that it had been in the heady days of the 1970s when Togo's phosphate, coffee, cocoa, and cotton prices had followed the world's oil prices upward. The government mortgaged the revenues from selling these commodities to build enormous tourist hotels and to indulge in other prestige economic development projects. Few of them were profitable. By the time Gilles arrived in Lomé, the opportunities were fewer and the potential rewards were smaller, but they were still more attractive than in Cotonou.

Gilles got a job with a Lebanese man who had a contract with the Ministry of Culture. He was paid less than a Peace Corps Volunteer's modest living allowance to help organize and promote dance and theater performances. Unlike the Volunteers, he was provided neither lodging nor any medical coverage. Gilles quickly determined that there was no fortune to be made in the entertainment business, but his small job supported him until he could find a better opportunity.

He was constantly looking for his chance, constantly scheming. Once, he tried to develop a lawn sod business on a farm in Adidogomé outside of Lomé. Later, he partnered with a Togolese friend in a neighborhood bar and *maquis* restaurant that was profitable only on a very small scale with no hope of expansion. He was perpetually seeking partners for his latest venture, where he would provide the idea and the direction and the potential partners--mostly Lebanese and Togolese businesspeople--would invest their money.

Gilles had no car and no motorcycle, nor even a moped. He didn't take regular taxis and pay the single person fare. Instead, he walked to the main routes and took the crowded 50 *franc* shared taxis. He even took the motorcycle taxis called *zemidjans* once they were introduced from Cotonou where they were popular.

Zemidjans could not have arrived in Lomé before the early 1990s political crisis. In the new atmosphere of struggle, people viewed the enforcement of helmet and traffic safety laws as a violation of human rights and individual freedom. The slumping economy added justification for the traffic anarchy. "Anything goes" became the rule on the streets. *Zemidjans* and other unorthodox means of travel became commonplace.

Riding the *zemidjans* and seeing their numbers grow gave Gilles the idea to enter the field. Chaos insured effortless entry into the transportation market. It was easy to avoid or ignore licenses and permits, saving time and money. He convinced a Lebanese associate, new to town from Beirut, to finance the purchase of a ragtag fleet of second- and third-hand motorcycles. He tried to run them according to the automobile taxi model. Each "driver" was supposed to buy his own gas and to bring Gilles a certain fixed amount of "rent" each day. They operated out of an open-air mechanics' shop where piles of broken-down motorcycles were strewn around the yard. They tried to scavenge enough parts from them to keep the fleet rolling.

The moto-taxi fleet died an agonizing death. The motorcycles, already in bad shape, began falling apart very quickly. The rent that Gilles received from the "drivers" was not enough to cover the parts and labor for the repairs. The motorcycles broke down so often and for such long periods that the drivers either abandoned them, disassembled them for parts to sell, or simply absconded with the ones that were in the best working condition. Soon, there was nothing remaining that was of any value.

Gilles rarely allowed his business disappointments get him down. He was usually bubbling over with enthusiasm and radiating confidence as he described his latest venture. He was occasionally given to melancholy, however, when something or someone caused him to pause and confront his lack of progress in realizing his dreams. One evening, he and I happened to be standing next to each other at the bar of "Le Bowling Alley" night club. We were staring at Fifi, a stunningly beautiful Lebanese eighteen-year-old. She was a new arrival in town, fresh from escaping the violent conflict that was raging in Beirut. She was surrounded by a crowd of European and Lebanese male admirers.

"A man like me," he said sadly. "What could I offer a young woman like Fifi? Nothing. What chance would I have with her? None. Ahhhhh, Fifi!"

Gilles never stayed down for long and soon he had a new interest. The regulars who played billiards at "Le Bowling Alley" included men who were fixtures of the local business community. Among them were diamond and gold merchants. Gilles was intrigued that they appeared to be prospering in spite of the fact that there were no diamonds to be found in Togo's mountains and only minuscule quantities of gold. Economic statistics, on the other hand, indicated the export of a considerable amount of both. The middle-aged men with whom he played billiards hardly seemed the type of swashbucklers and adventurers that he imagined smugglers to be.

Smuggling was an important part of the Togolese economy, but most people did not know how it worked. Not only gold and diamonds but also a significant portion of Togo's cocoa and coffee exports had their origins in Ghana. In Togo, the owners received payment in a "hard" convertible currency, the *franc CFA* that was backed by the French *franc,* instead of in the Ghanaian currency, the *cedi,* that was practically worthless at the artificial fixed rate of exchange. For those who pilfered from the mines where they worked or used rudimentary tools to dig on their own, the prospect of much better remuneration for their efforts made smuggling their diamonds or gold out of the country worth the risk. Coffee and cocoa buyers were often motivated to smuggle their purchases out of Ghana rather than selling them to official exporters for the same reasons. Underpaid customs officials were ripe for bribery, making them essential partners in the smuggling enterprise.

The smell of gold and diamonds could not escape the notice of an ambitious fellow like Gilles. It was not long before he began cultivating the friendship of one of his billiards acquaintances, Jean-Paul. A Frenchman of Tunisian-Jewish origin, he was a long-established diamond merchant in Lomé. Gilles asked Jean-Paul how his business worked and found him to be surprisingly candid in his response.

"In Togo, I'm a legitimate businessman," Jean-Paul explained. "I am registered. I pay my taxes fully and properly."

"But aren't you a smuggler?" asked Gilles.

"Absolutely not," he replied. "I have never transported diamonds or gold from Ghana into Togo and I never will."

"You travel to Ghana regularly, don't you?" asked Gilles.

"Yes," said Jean-Paul. "I make contacts and arrange transactions but I never consummate the deal there. I never smuggle anything out of Ghana. That would be illegal. People bring me gold and diamonds in Lomé that I buy and send off to Europe. It's all very above-board and legal."

Jean-Paul's story delighted Gilles. The process appeared to be enormously profitable--the fast track to wealth that he had been looking for.

"It sounds so simple, almost fool-proof," said Gilles.

"It is simple," Jean-Paul continued. "But I follow a few rules and I never waver from them. I never touch any merchandise in Ghana. I never transport anything across the borders. I always pay my taxes. I always insure and ship my parcels to Europe using the best air courier services. I send with the Belgian airline most of the time, so that my customers in the diamond market in Antwerp can easily pick up their purchases at the airport in Brussel;s. I never hide what I am doing from the Togolese authorities. Finally, I make sure that the authorities are appropriately compensated."

Jean-Paul's *modus operandi* insured him against short-term loss because he only paid for the diamonds or gold upon delivery in Lomé. He examined and tested the merchandise with his expert eyes before any money changed hands.

Jean-Paul was impressed with Gilles and decided to try him out as an assistant. In no time, Gilles' enthusiasm and ambition blurred his judgment. He made several trips to Accra for Jean-Paul with uneventful border crossings. As a result, he decided that a "side deal" of his own would hurt nothing and would accelerate his rise into a life of wealth and comfort.

"At the border," he explained to the new backers whom he had recruited to front him the money for a diamond purchase, "the police and customs agents on both sides know me, just like they know my boss. I can cross without being searched. It's a great opportunity."

Gilles was surprised when, having violated most of Jean-Paul's cardinal rules in his "side deal," he was subjected for the first time to a thorough search at the border on his return from Accra and was arrested in possession of diamonds.

The Ghanaian customs inspectors took his backpack, including the packet of diamonds, and led him to an empty room. They seated him on a hardback chair directly under a bare light bulb dangling from the ceiling and closed the door. He remained in the room for several hours and no one entered.

Finally, he heard Jean-Paul's voice in the hallway.

"Your employee is in big trouble, my friend," came the voice of the Chief Customs Officer. "Diamonds are a precious resource for our country. Stealing them is a very serious offense."

"He is not my employee," he heard Jean-Paul say. "He is just an acquaintance. He is my countryman. When I heard that he was in difficulty, I wanted to find out where he was and what was his status--for humanitarian reasons."

"Of course," replied the Customs man.

Gilles heard them walking down the hall. A half-hour later, they returned and entered the room.

"You are a lucky man," said Jean-Paul on entering. "Very foolish, but very lucky nonetheless. You have broken Ghanaian law, but since this is your first time, the chief has decided to let you go with a warning. Let's go."

"Thank you," said Gilles to the chief as he followed Jean-Paul out the door.

As they exited the Customs office, Gilles picked up his backpack. On the way to the car, he opened it.

"The parcel is gone," he exclaimed as he stopped in his tracks.

Jean-Paul turned around and glared at Gilles.

"You're lucky to be free," he said. "The mercy of our friend, the Chief, has its limits. Get in the car."

Jean-Paul was seething with anger and said nothing as they drove across the border. He clenched his teeth, stared straight ahead, and gripped the steering wheel tightly. On the Togo side, the police and customs officers simply waved them through without stopping. A hundred meters past the border, Jean-Paul pulled over to the side of the road and stopped.

"You idiot! Do you know what you've done?" he yelled at Gilles. "Why couldn't you just follow my instructions?"

Gilles tried to utter an apology, but Jean-Paul cut him short.

"I have spent years building my business and building a reputation for honesty and dependability," he said. "In one day, you have damaged my business more than any competitor."

Jean-Paul was furious almost to the point of shaking.

"In order to make this embarrassment go away and try to minimize the damage to my reputation, I had to grease the palms of the Ghanaian Customs officers to get you released. I will have to pay off your investors for the loss of their diamonds in order to salvage my reputation, even though you acted without my knowledge or approval."

He paused and then spat out, "Get out of my car and never come near me again!"

The effect of Gilles' fiasco on Jean-Paul's business was devastating. Ghanaian diamond-sellers lost confidence in Jean-Paul because of Gilles' actions. Sellers who had gone to Jean-Paul for years began going to some of his new competitors among the Indian merchants in town. Jean-Paul knew that Gilles was not able to repay him and probably never would be. He had no choice but to write off the loss and to confront the increased competition from the Indians.

Gilles kept a low profile for the next few months but it was no mean feat. Lomé was not a huge city and the expatriate community was small and incestuous. He left town for a while and began visiting a series of European friends and acquaintances in the interior of the country--priests and brothers, technical aid workers, road-builders, volunteers with non-governmental organizations, regional managers of commercial houses, and teachers. Each visit was timed to be short enough that his hosts enjoyed the change in company but not long enough to wear out his welcome.

Everyone was surprised a few months later when Gilles reappeared in Lomé and began to work for Joseph, an African-American businessman. Beginning in the early 1960s, Joseph ran a travel agency that specialized in guiding tour groups of African-Americans eager to visit and learn about the land of their ancestors.

Joseph needed to diversify his activities to compensate for slumps in travel to Africa due to fuel price spikes, political upheavals, and wars on the continent. Money-changing was a natural complement to the travel business. It was something that travelers, resident expatriates, and businesspeople needed to do and for which the local banks were inefficient and expensive. He carefully and slowly built a foreign exchange business that many people came to rely upon. In particular, the Americans, Canadians, and Anglophone Africans in the foreign community and among the travelers transiting through Lomé preferred to do business with him. As with his counterparts in the gold and diamond business, the authorities knew of his business and were well-compensated.

"If you are legal, why do you need to pay off the authorities?" Gilles asked Joseph.

"Because, my friend, there is no predictable application of law here," replied Joseph. "My business is legal, yes, but this government doesn't understand business or the law. Do you know what one high official told me? 'All businessmen are thieves!' They don't know how to manage their own affairs properly and they don't know how to tax fairly. When the government needs money, sometimes they tell each businessman to bring a certain amount of money on a certain date or risk having his business shut down by the authorities. Paying key people helps protect me from these arbitrary attacks."

"Why do you think your French brothers only do restaurants and bars and don't invest in industries?" he continued. "Because they like food and wine? No. It's the business that is most profitable but involves the least risk and draws the least attention from the government."

Competition was ferocious in the local foreign exchange market. The arrival of Indian merchants on the scene had further complicated the foreign exchange market just as it had upset the diamond and gold markets. For the first time in decades, there was a real challenge to the domination of the entrenched merchants.

Joseph was satisfied with Gilles' work with the tours. Gilles, however, wanted to get involved in the more lucrative foreign exchange part of the business. Joseph would not agree. He had been burned recently. One day, without warning and without explanation, the customs officers at the airport had seized a package of cash that he was sending to deposit in a European bank. Since the money transfer was perfectly legal, Joseph repeatedly tried to recuperate his money for months after the seizure but to no avail.

Joseph eventually learned that some of his competitors had tipped-off the customs agents to the shipment and arranged for it to be seized. Gilles knew about the shipment and bragged about it to some of the Indian businessmen with whom he was cultivating a relationship. They exploited his information to their benefit and nearly caused Joseph to go bankrupt in the process.

Joseph fired Gilles as soon as he found what he had done.

"That boy Gilles could screw up a free lunch, you know?" Joseph told me one day when I tried to change money with him and he was unable to do so. He could do nothing but shake his head in resignation.

"I'll never trust anyone ever again," he vowed.

"This was a good business," he concluded. "If he had just kept his mouth shut instead of trying to impress people, he could have earned a good living. I did, at least until he came along."

It was information that Joseph gave to Gilles, however, that led him to Jacqueline and her restaurant.

When I was on a business trip back to Lomé, Gilles waited on me at my table at one of the city's finest French restaurants. He acted as if he owned the place. He didn't know that I knew that he waited tables there, and more, for Jacqueline, the Frenchwoman who had been the owner for more than twenty years. He slept with her and worked for her at the restaurant and kept her company. She kept him on a monthly allowance.

Gilles' mistress was a handsome woman--what the Togolese called "a woman of substance." Her three grown sons by three different fathers were in the same age group as Gilles.

Gilles was of average height and slight build compared to her. His prematurely gray hair and the air of officiousness that he had adopted aided the ruse that he was her equal partner, but everyone knew that he was a "kept man." Behind their backs, the couple's friends and acquaintances referred to him as her "poodle."

Jacqueline seemed immune to Gilles' periodic proposals that she fund his latest scheme. She was amused by them, as she would be if they were proposed by one of her sons.

"Don't worry," she assured him when a new idea revealed itself to be unworkable. "I'll take care of you."

Jacqueline's best friend, Chantal, was the proprietor of *Le Paradis*, a popular nightclub, for more than two decades. A Frenchwoman of the same age as Jacqueline, she was thin and chic. Chantal was, in principle, bisexual, but no one could remember her having a lover who was not a young woman. She had first come to Africa with a husband who worked for a road-building company. His job kept him away from home for months at a time. This and the fact that they had no children left her with time to pursue her own business and amorous interests. The husband was out of the picture for so long that no one could remember him except Jacqueline.

When the club closed in the early hours each morning, she and the attractive young Togolese and Ghanaian women who worked for her as bartenders and servers retired to her nearby home to unwind and eat breakfast. When Chantal didn't have a "steady" girlfriend, the girls took turns staying with her for the remainder of the night and the morning.

For a long time, Chantal had been proposing to Jacqueline that the two of them should prepare to return home to France to live out their lives together. At first, Jacqueline was ambivalent about Chantal's entreaties. She had never considered herself bisexual let alone lesbian but she could not imagine herself being on more intimate terms with anyone than she was with Chantal.

The illness of Jacqueline's elderly mother in France intervened in her life. Over a period of more than a year, she traveled frequently to aid her siblings in the care of their mother. Each time, she left Gilles to run the restaurant. She called him daily from France to give him instructions and to make sure that he did not take advantage of her absence to do something foolish.

Her mother's slow dying made her begin to think about her own mortality. Chantal's proposal became very attractive to her. Finally, Jacqueline agreed that they would embark upon a new stage of life together--a stage where

Gilles and Chantal's girlfriends had no place. With no mention to Gilles, she pooled her savings with that of Chantal. They purchased and furnished a home together in Montpellier, a city in the south of France six miles inland from the coast of the Mediterranean. Chantal sold *Le Paradis* first and moved to their new home.

Word of the death of Jacqueline's mother came while Gilles was off visiting Northern Togo and Burkina Faso. He had been trying to convince Jacqueline that the large number of expatriate aid workers and businesspeople traveling through the area indicated that a restaurant and small hotel in the north would be a profitable enterprise. He was scouting possible sites all along the northern reaches of National Road Number 1 and the road into Burkina Faso.

By the time Gilles returned to Lomé, Jacqueline was gone. In her place, he found Bernard, a Frenchman in his early 70s, an "old Africa hand." He was tall, fit, and tan, with steel-gray hair combed straight back from his forehead and wore wire-rimmed aviator sunglasses. He had retired twice-- once from the government colonial service and then again from a company that contracted with the French cooperation agency after the independence of France's African colonies.

Gilles was stunned to learn that Bernard was the new owner of the restaurant.

"I can't live in France anymore," Bernard explained to Gilles as they sat down on the terrace to have a drink. "I've been here too long. I might as well be one of them, the Africans."

Gilles was dazed. He stared at the two tall glasses of cool water into which Bernard stirred *pastis* liqueur, immediately turning the drinks milky white. He had assumed that he would "inherit" the restaurant when Jacqueline finally returned to France. Now, his future that had been clear as water was as cloudy as the drinks in front of him. Finally he spoke.

"She always said that she would take care of me," he murmured.

"And so she did," Bernard replied. "In addition to your room and board, you'll have good wages. Jacqueline assured me that you are the best waiter that she ever had!"

SUPI

"My lesbian friend?" Afi exclaimed indignantly as she sat up in bed. "Adjoa is not a lesbian. We don't have lesbians in Africa--that's just for the Europeans. After all, she's married and has two children."

"I don't know what else to call a woman who makes love to another woman," said Mensah.

"You don't understand her," she explained. "Adjoa is my friend. Just because she leaves me so excited and frustrated after her visits that I have to let the likes of you into my bed doesn't mean that she is a lesbian.

"You don't know about this because you are a man," she continued. "Back in the days of our parents and grandparents, women knew how to help each other. When a husband was traveling for hunting, or trade, or war, or even when he was spending most of his time with a new young wife, what could a woman do? Find a boy or a man? What would happen if a husband returned to find his wife pregnant? We women learned how to comfort each other."

"I'm sorry for being insensitive," Mensah replied. "And I don't mean to be unkind to her. But remember, I'm your friend, too. While I enjoy the 'leftovers' from her meals--and I am grateful for them, truly I am--I didn't create the situation. Adjoa did. You know very well that it is not acceptable among our people for a man to lie down with a woman and satiate himself and then to leave his woman unsatisfied. If she's going to 'play the man' with you, she should not leave you unsatisfied. It's not right."

"You are such an ass, Mensah," said Afi with annoyance as she got up from bed and wrapped her cloth around her. "If she didn't leave me so hot every week, when would you ever find someone to have sex with you?

"She and I have been doing this for a long time," Afi continued with exasperation. "And I enjoy what we do. When she comes to visit, she always wants to lie down on the bed with me and talk. Then, she begins to wrestle with me. The more I resist, the more aroused she becomes and the more she insists until I give in. She's bigger and stronger than me. You know how worked up I am by the time she leaves. I enjoy our playing but I just haven't been able to have an orgasm with her for a long time. I try, but sometimes I have to pretend. I'm just happy that she gets some relief with me from the stresses of her life.

"Anyway, I'm glad you're here," she said. "I trust you even if you can be insufferable at times. Otherwise, God knows what diseased creature I might drag into my room."

"It's great for me," Mensah grinned. "It's not every day that a beautiful woman drags me into her room yelling, 'Do me! Do me! Please do me now!' I know that it's hard to believe, but you're the only one."

"Go away and leave me alone," she laughed. "I need to rest. But don't leave me alone next Saturday!"

"Never. I'm very reliable, no?"

Afi's relationship with Adjoa began when they met at boarding secondary school in Ghana. Adjoa was a year older than Afi. Both were from families that were arbitrarily separated by the international boundary with Togo or, as the saying went, they "slept on Ghana side and bathed on Togo side." They gravitated toward each other and became good friends. Adjoa had a very pretty face, was outgoing, even a bit aggressive, with a tall and athletic build. If no one was watching, she would playfully pin Afi against a wall or a doorway and rub her body against the younger girl. It was all in good fun and these little incidents began and ended quickly in laughter.

"You will be my *Supi*," Adjoa often reminded her. Afi came to accept, and was proud of, the idea that she would be the older girl's "*Supi* wife" when the time came.

No one knows exactly when "*Supi* marriages" began. Certainly, it was an unintended consequence of the system of boarding secondary schools created during the British colonial period. Boarding school was a thoroughly British institution that intended to create an indigenous elite that was imbued with the culture and the values of Britain.

The girls simply carried their customary practice with them to the dormitories and adapted it to their needs. In boarding schools, the senior girls who were preparing for their examinations would "marry" an underclass girl, who became her "*Supi* wife." In order to free the senior to study for exams, the "wife" did all her chores--cooking, cleaning, laundry, and drawing water. "*Supi* marriages" were publicly perceived as innocent and non-sexual, so much so that teachers and school authorities sometimes attended the "wedding ceremonies" and blessed the "*Supi* marriage." The girls were discreet and the possibility of a sexual relationship remained unspoken. This allowed parents and teachers to overlook the practice even when they were conscious of it.

At the beginning of each school year, there was always an intense

                    Kelly J. Morris

competition among the senior girls for "*Supi* wives." It was a foregone conclusion, however, that once Adjoa entered her final examination year, she would take Afi as her "*Supi* wife." A "*Supi* wife" could not refuse any request by her "husband." Therefore, Afi did not refuse when Adjoa created a tent by hanging sheets around the bottom level of her dormitory room double-decker bed and called Afi to join her there. The "*Supi* couples" took turns serving as sentinel for each other in case a teacher or the headmistress should be approaching while they were having sex.

The girls in the dormitory were comfortable with *Supi*, whether their *Supi* marriages included sex or not. Sexual activity was done in fun. The affections that the girls professed for each other and expressed sexually were easily transferred to their boyfriends during during school holidays and to their boyfriends and husbands when they finally departed the all-female environment of boarding school. The emotional attachments and jealousies of some of the couples, however, were as intense as any male-female relationship.

Unfortunately, after one active love-making session together at the end of the school year, Afi began bleeding heavily. They rushed her to the clinic and it did not take the doctor long to ascertain what had occurred that provoked the bleeding.

Word spread quickly about Afi's injury. In no time, it led to yet another round of public controversy about *Supi* in the Ghanaian tabloid press. In news articles and in "Letters to the Editor," the names of the two girls and that of their school were not cited but members of the community denounced the practice of "*Supi* marriages." They described *Supi* as an intimate friendship between two girls at boarding schools where one of the girls played the role of "boy-friend" and they slept together in one bed. Without indulging in clinical descriptions, they made it quite clear that more than sleep was going on.

"Halt this evil practice!" intoned one letter to the *Ghanaian Daily Telegraph*. "I call upon all women's associations, churches, and parents organizations to stop this debauched practice. Like the Ghanaian girls prostituting themselves in foreign cities, these girls are dragging the good name of Ghanaian women in the mud."

"These girls must be made to control their passions," wrote another reader to the *Talking Drums*. "If they cannot control themselves for the length of the school term, how will they control themselves once they are married and their husbands must travel?"

"The Apostle Paul wrote to the Romans," wrote a pastor, "condemning that 'their women did change the natural use unto that which is against nature.' He called their acts 'vile affections.' It is an affront to God's law! These girls must desist for the sake of their souls."

"Once they find out that a girl is practicing *Supi*," added yet another in the *Accra Weekly Herald*, "it will drive away potential suitors. No man wants to marry a lesbian."

Still other correspondents called *Supi* "disgraceful," "immoral," and "un-African." Many writers were less concerned that these oversexed schoolgirls might become homosexual and more concerned that their uncontrollable desires might lead them to succumb to prostitution instead of a life as wife and mother. For them, *Supi* was a "slippery slope" leading to harlotry.

"*Supism*" was not without its defenders.

"These letters to the newspapers about *Supi* do nothing but repeat a bunch of made-up lies!" a woman replied in *The Progressive Ghanaian*. "They are unfairly tarnishing the reputation of these schoolgirls. The friendship between girls in '*Supi* marriages' is not so extreme as these letter-writers would have your readers believe. It is a perfectly innocent way for junior students to relieve the senior students of some of their housekeeping duties so that they can prepare for exams. There is nothing more. These hysterical tales are nothing but rubbish."

One intrepid anonymous letter-writer even dared to defend *Supi* as a safe way for young girls to explore their sexuality and relieve stress without risking pregnancy or disease and without becoming committed lesbians. This set off a heated exchange about whether or not the *Supi* practitioners were truly lesbians if they eventually abandoned the practice and married a man.

Adjoa and Afi were not allowed to return to school in September. Both girls crossed into Togo to finish their schooling. After perfecting her French, Afi was able to salvage a successful career and went on to graduate from the university. She was, after all, considered to be the "victim" of a sexually aggressive older girl who "bullied" her into a lesbian relationship. Adjoa also caught up in French but her education was cut short.

"It's not fair," Afi had protested. "I was not a victim. We were just playing. It was an accident!"

No one wanted to listen to her.

"It's best just to get on with your life," her parents admonished her.

Eventually, Adjoa was able to qualify as an English teacher at a junior secondary school. It was not long before she married a fellow teacher and quickly had two children. When Adjoa's husband later learned that there was a lesbian incident in her past, he was upset.

"What man wants a wife who is a lesbian," he whined, "or who cannot control her sexual urges?"

Adjoa quieted him by saying, "Would you have preferred that I played the harlot with all the boys and men? I did not do it. I saved myself for my husband."

Adjoa had carefully chosen a husband who was gullible, timid, less intelligent than her, and easily bullied. He needed to have a second income in the family that matched his own income. In the end, it was easier for him to accept her story that *Supi* allowed her to save herself for him than to contemplate the idea that his wife might prefer women as lovers.

Afi and Adjoa remained friends over the years. Like many other *Supi* couples, they continued their sexual relationship even after Adjoa married and had children. Afi might not have agreed to continue the sex but she felt bad that her friend's education had been truncated while she had the opportunity to continue. Acceding to Adjoa's desires was a way to comfort her friend and salve her own sense of guilt. Adjoa, for her part, feared injuring her friend again. Still, they both looked forward to Saturday mornings when Adjoa would leave her unsuspecting husband and two children in the company of the maid and visit Afi at her small apartment.

Afi and Mensah both lived in a compound adjacent to the lagoon that separated the sandbar on which "old Lomé" was situated and the red clay escarpment where the new quarters and suburbs were located. Inside the compound, there were several "trains"--long, narrow block-wall, zinc-roof buildings that were divided into two-room apartments. They were whitewashed inside and out with tints of yellow, blue, and green ochre. Afi lived in an end unit and Mensah lived next door to her.

Each apartment consisted of a front and back room. Young working people--singles or couples--used the inner room as a bedroom. They used the outer room as a sitting and eating area. There would be a food preparation table with a bottled gas burner, a small refrigerator, pots, pans, and porcelain-covered metal serving and storage bowls. Across from this area, one would find a couch, a couple of chairs, and large coffee table that doubled as a dining table. Those who preferred charcoal could cook on a grill outside in front of the apartment. One bare bulb dangling from the ceiling illuminated each room. A Chinese-made standing fan, a battery-operated radio, and perhaps a small black-and-white television typically completed the scene. Families with children might rent two adjacent units. Outside spigots were the water source and the renters shared bucket-shower stalls and toilets.

Mensah enjoyed teasing Afi about her long-time "friend." He was careful, however, never to make her angry enough to cut him off from the enjoyment of Adjoa's "leftovers." Mensah and Afi had grown up near each other and their families were friends and distantly related. He was a year older than her. When Mensah was in his teens, it was Afi's older cousin, Akossiwa, who had initiated Mensah into the world of sex.

Young people grew up among a gaggle of neighbors, friends, and cousins of varying proximity. It was among them that they had the first dawning of their sexuality and eventually their first sexual experiences. Girls grew up bathing together, touching and embracing each other, dancing and wrestling, and often sleeping together in groups. During January nights when the *Harmattan* wind from the desert was particularly strong, Afi and her teenage friends and cousins huddled together on mattresses and cushions under cloths and blankets to keep each other warm and ward off the cold. It was all considered to be perfectly innocent. Most of the time, it was.

This is the way it had always been among young people. No one ever thought about what label would apply to a girl who expressed her affection for another girl, let alone how doing so might change the course of her life, limit her options, or cause her disappointment and pain.

The changes first came from the fulminations of fire and brimstone of Pentacostalist and Charismatic ministers who stirred up fear, hatred, and revulsion towards male homosexuality and lesbianism. *Supi* was the object of condemnation to hellfire. Why natural, spontaneous, and discreet behavior should suddenly be characterized as undermining the morals of Ghanaian women was difficult for Afi and her peers to understand. The fact that these preachers judged these actions and put labels on those who indulged in them was insidious rather than the practices themselves. The idea of lesbianism and the label of lesbian never even existed before these preachers, mired in the Nineteenth Century theology of European missionaries and the new Pentacostalists and charismatics from North America, began demonizing same-sex affection.

Mensah was the one who initiated Afi to male-female sex. A distant cousin, he was more experienced than she was but not by much. She was grateful for the relaxed and gentle manner that he had with her after the "first time" horror stories of some of her classmates. Even in his teens, Mensah was a persistent and frequently obnoxious tease. Underneath this exterior, however, Afi came to know Mensah as an intelligent, perceptive, and trustworthy person. After his secondary school studies in Togo and some training programs in Europe and in other African countries, he worked at the Ministry of Rural Development.

Afi considered herself lucky that Mensah had tipped her off to the little apartment next door to him. After she graduated from the university and started her professional career, she felt secure to have a friend from home living next door. When the need arose, there was no one else that she could have trusted to satisfy her sexual needs without the burden of a "relationship" and without fear of disease or pregnancy. The only price that she had to pay was to put up with his relentless teasing. He could and did say just about anything to provoke and to elicit a response from whomever was his interlocutor. Fortunately, she knew exactly how to handle him from years of practice. She did not back down and gave as good as she got.

After three years working at the Ministry of Social Affairs and Women's Development, Afi was delighted to receive a scholarship to go to the United

States for a Master's degree in Public Health. She was so excited that she did not notice at first the effect that her impending departure was having on Adjoa. The prospect of going two or more years without seeing her lover triggered a crisis with Adjoa. She became very emotional and their Saturday morning sessions became increasingly dramatic and tearful as the departure date approached. Adjoa begged her not to leave. Once, she became hysterical and threatened to kill herself. Another time, she became angry and warned Afi that, when she returned, she would find Adjoa in the arms of another woman.

As much as Afi cared for Adjoa, it was obvious that Adjoa's feelings ran much deeper than hers. Adjoa blurted out her own feelings of guilt that she had been carrying for years. Afi had never become pregnant in the years since the dormitory incident, even though she had never lacked for male companionship at the university and afterwards and had been surprisingly slow to practice contraception.

"I fear that the hurt that I caused you at school may have made you unable to conceive," Adjoa admitted.

Afi was stunned. She had never thought about the possibility that she might be sterile. She had just assumed that she was lucky. Contemplating the possibility of a childless future caused her to call into question many of her hopes and plans. Whatever her relationship with Adjoa, she had never doubted for a minute that one day she would marry a man, settle down, and have children.

"How did I avoid getting pregnant before I began to use contraceptives," she wondered. "Am I infertile? I don't remember any illnesses or infections while I was growing up that could have had such dire consequences. If I am sterile, did the 'incident' cause it?"

It was a time of change for Afi. She was trying to situate herself and to sort out how she was feeling before she continued her studies and pursued her professional goals. She tried to locate herself along the spectrum of gender roles and sexual orientation and sexual identity--something that she never felt the need to do previously. It did not help matters that a new straight-to-video movie industry had appeared on the scene. In many of the videos made in Nigeria and Ghana that were becoming ubiquitous, the "evil lesbian" was a stock character--a violent, criminal, mad character who always meets a terrible fate, often dragging her "victim" with her. As traumatic as the uproar around the "incident" had been, this transition was even more challenging.

Afi was exasperated with Mensah.

"Why do you or anyone else need to label a person because of their sexuality?" she asked. "Why can't people just accept others for who they are and what they are?"

While her tolerance of Mensah's teasing was wearing thin, they remained close friends. Mensah was the person who was most honest with her. She counted on him to tell her exactly what he thought and exactly how she was viewed by those around her. In spite of the teasing, she knew that he accepted her unconditionally.

"I wish I could think of nothing but pursuing my studies," Afi complained to Mensah, "and adjusting to living in America. What will people think of me? What label is going to be pinned on me just for being myself. How will people act towards me?

"My departure is causing Adjoa a great deal of pain," she continued.

"She's not threatening to kill herself again, is she?" asked Mensah sympathetically.

"No, that part has passed, thank God," she responded. "She will survive this, but she is terribly sad. I promised to keep in touch and not forget her.

She has her husband and her children and the rest of the family, as well as her friends and her fellow teachers. She will never be lacking for company. It is only with me, however, that she has shared a secret part of herself that no one else knows. Even surrounded by people, she will still be lonely in certain ways. I would like to think that she could find someone else--another woman--with whom she could share that private part of herself and be intimate with, someone to comfort her and be comforted. To tell you the truth, Mensah, if I felt the need for a new relationship with a woman in this town, I wouldn't know where to start looking."

"You're no longer in a dormitory full of girls, that's true," said Mensah, "but I'm sure that she will find someone."

Mensah accompanied her from Lomé to Kotoka International Airport in Accra. Her flight would take her to New York where she would be met by some relatives. A few days later, she would take a flight to Southern California. While waiting out a weather delay in the departure lounge, Mensah and Afi reminisced and talked about her upcoming studies and her impending two-year stint in California or, as Mensah insisted on calling it, Hollywood.

"Mensah, not all of California is Hollywood," she scolded him. "Who knows? I may never set foot in Hollywood while I'm there."

"You won't be far from it," he insisted. "You'll be close enough to Hollywood to find a new lover-girl in no time at all. I read that it is a very fashionable thing to do there, whether you are lesbian or not."

"Will you never change?" she exploded. "Is there nothing but pornography showing on that movie screen in your brain? Why do you care so much about women together? What if I find a boyfriend? What if I just throw myself into my studies and have no time for a lover at all?"

"Don't be so angry," he replied laughing. "You know that I just can't help teasing you. It was like that when we were children, wasn't it? Why should it be different now?"

"You should be grown-up and mature by now," she replied sternly.

"Besides," he continued. "you're not the only one to lie down with someone of the same sex. I did, too."

"What!" Afi exclaimed. "You hypocrite! I didn't know that you had gay sex. You're bisexual after all!"

"Gay? Bisexual? Absolutely not. Look who is the hypocrite now-- applying labels to people!" he insisted. "It was just for money. The year that I spent in Accra to take accountancy courses, there was a British man who was very friendly with me. One evening, he invited me to one of the big luxury hotels for dinner and then to the bar to drink and dance. Finally, he invited me up to his room. He wanted to 'be a woman' for me. As long as I 'play the man,' it's not gay so I agreed. He was very kind and generous to me. I got my pleasure like I would with a woman. Why not? After that first time, he used to leave his wife and children at home once or twice a week to spend the evening with me at the hotel."

"What became of him?" asked Afi. She was still shocked by her friend's unexpected revelation.

"Things came to a pretty abrupt end," he said.

"His wife found out?" she asked.

"His wife already knew that he was bisexual ever since his days in boarding school. The British don't care about such matters, especially the upper-class ones," he replied. "No doubt she also had a lover. One night, we heard a ruckus outside the hotel in the parking lot and we looked out the window. The harlot girls from the hotel bar were having a humbug on my friend. They were angry with him for taking a boy to his room instead of one of them. To teach him a lesson, they set his car on fire and burnt it to the ground! It frightened him so much that he packed up his family and went straightaway back to Britain. Such a shame--it was a nice white Peugeot car."

"Mensah, you are incorrigible," Afi said as she shook her head.

The flight to New York was finally announced. Her friend Mensah merited a tight embrace good-bye before she walked down the corridor to the plane.

As her plane lifted off the runway and headed in the direction of New York, Afi settled back in her seat. She was relieved to be alone with her own thoughts. She reflected on the changes taking place, the expectations of the people in her life, and her discomfort with the labels pinned on her. She wondered if she would ever have a child.

"When I was in school," she recalled, "*Supi* was how girls supported and comforted and showed affection to each other. Just a few years later, it has become the Ghanaian word for 'lesbian.'

"The original meaning of *Supi* is different. *Supi* refers to a stool. Each one of us when we are born is given a stool. It's there that your spirit sits. It is unique to you and different from any other person. It is where you are located.

"I think I like that definition best," she thought. "The stool where my spirit sits is only for me and not for anyone else. It is constant. I can come back to it for the rest of my life."

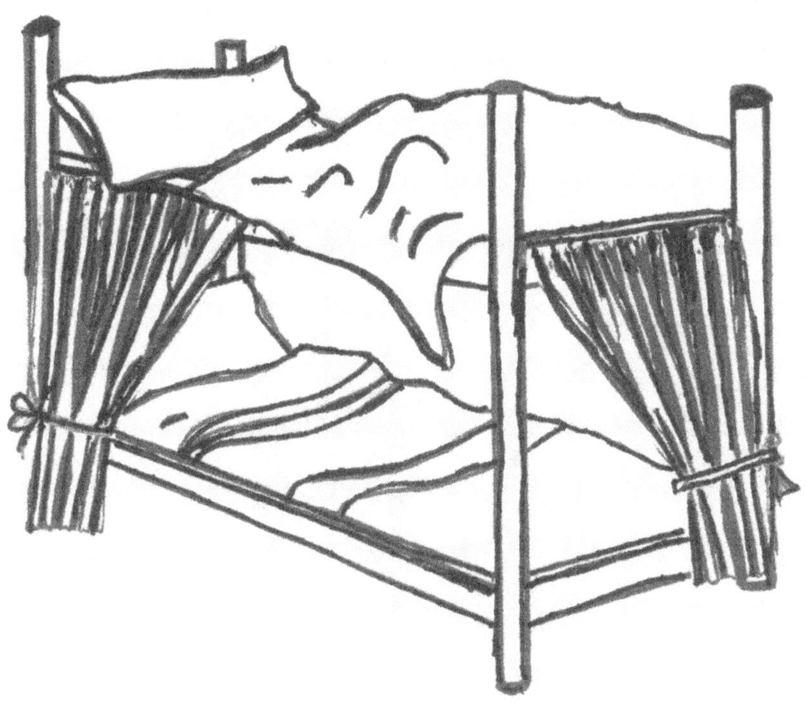

AFRICHOCO

"Let me get this straight," Kenneth asked. "You grow coffee and cocoa for sale but you never drink or eat either one?"

"Yes, we grow them just to sell," replied Kojovi, the spokesman for the group of young planters that Kenneth was visiting. "It is not our habit to drink hot beverages at home."

Kenneth hesitated a moment and reflected before continuing. He was a young Briton working for the UN Food and Agriculture Organization. An agricultural economist and agribusiness specialist, he aimed for a successful career at FAO, early retirement, and a much more profitable second career in coffee and cocoa agribusiness--perhaps with Nestlé, Cadbury, or Hershey. He had begun visiting Togo regularly from his regional base in Abidjan to advise the government's coffee and cocoa promotion agency.

"I have come to the conclusion," he said, "that in this country, planters are not interested in transforming their crops to add value and get a better price and more profit before selling for export. Neither are they interested in making a product to be sold on the the local market to replace imported goods. They just grow the coffee and cocoa, harvest it, dry it, bag it, and sell it to produce buyers. Am I right?"

The young planters and their families who had assembled for Kenneth's visit nodded their heads tentatively, unsure of where his discourse was headed.

"And they are content to receive a pittance compared to what their crops will earn the middlemen and the government on the world market. Am I right again?"

The young people stirred uncomfortably until one of them stood and spoke.

"We're not content to receive this pittance, as you call it, but what choice do we have?" he said with more than a touch of irritation in his voice.

Kenneth ignored the question and continued.

"Nobody is interested in making anything," he said, matching the young man's indignant tone with his own. "At most, people in this country want to import goods from other countries, pay bribes to avoid or reduce customs duties, and resell on the local market. The margin of profit is the taxes that they do not pay. "

The group stirred and buzzed with conversation.

"For someone who has spent so little time in our country," another participant joined in, "you are very quick to make these vast generalizations about it. We're a small nation, but we're not so easy to understand as you seem to think."

"Perhaps you're right," he replied, "but I have eyes to see, a mouth to ask questions, ears to hear the answers, and a mind to analyze them. I have traveled the length of this country several times. In every marketplace, at every lorry park and stand, along every street, there is someone who has set up wooden benches and a charcoal stove where he sells hot coffee or cocoa mixed with sweetened condensed milk. People dunk their *baguettes* in it or accompany their omelets with it. If a worker on the way to his job or a traveler has little money and doesn't want to drink a shot or two of *sodabi*, what is his alternative? Togolese coffee and cocoa are sold cheaply to foreigners who process them and package them into consumer products that increase their profits. And if Togolese want to buy these products like instant coffee or powdered cocoa made with Togolese coffee and cocoa that they sold so cheaply, they pay dearly to get them. Am I right or not?"

The group became agitated. It spontaneously dissolved into smaller groups. Their animated discussions in Éwé were punctuated by gestures and occasional eruptions of loud arguments. Some of the participants stood and prepared to leave.

Kenneth observed the scene attentively but silently. He waited and spoke again only when the participants seemed ready to leave.

"Are you angry with what I have said," he asked, "or even with me personally?"

"Yes," was the chorus of responses. "Yes to both questions!"

"Good," Kenneth replied with satisfaction. "I didn't come here to flatter you or to talk about how you valiant farmers are the backbone of the country and all that."

Kenneth was treading dangerously close to mocking one of the ruling party's most sacred political slogans.

"I came here," he continued, "to make you angry, to make you indignant, but mostly to convince you to take the chance to do something different."

"We planters have been doing things differently from the other farmers in this country for three generations," replied Kojovi who was an articulate and obviously well-educated young man. "Coffee and cocoa are not native to our country. Our grandfathers cleared the mountain land under the tall shade trees to plant the coffee and cocoa seedlings. After 20 or 25 years, when the trees were beginning to produce less, the agency's extension agents convinced us to cut them down and plant new hybrid seedlings and to plant hybrid citrus and mangoes and other fruit trees, too. We did--some of us quicker than others. We know about taking a chance to do something different that may be more profitable to us. But we can't bring a Nestlé factory here. Can you? What is this 'something different' that you think that we should do?"

"No, I can't bring a Nestlé factory here," Kenneth replied, "but I may be able to help you build mini-factories."

All eyes and ears were directed to Kenneth.

"Here's what I propose," Kenneth announced. "First, a little background. Before I came to West and Central Africa, I was stationed for several years in the Caribbean, mainly in Trinidad and Tobago. They not only grow and export coffee and cocoa like you, but they also drink hot coffee and cocoa from their own produce. This is no doubt part of their colonial heritage from the British. They call all hot drinks tea and all alcoholic drinks are rum. There are several steps in the transformation from cocoa to chocolate that I picked up from my friends in Trinidad. The first ones you already do, but then they do things differently.

"Like you, they harvest the yellow and red cocoa pods by hand. Then they cut them in half with a *coupe-coupe*, remove the hard bitter seeds in their sweet white membranes, and let them ferment for six days. At the end of this time, the seed is less bitter if you bite into it. It's beginning to taste like chocolate. Finally, they spread the seeds out and dry them in the sun. When they are dry, the last of the sweet white membrane is gone.

"At this stage, you would normally grade the seeds and bag them in 100 kilogram sacks to sell to the produce buyers, correct?"

"Yes, that's how we do it," the group agreed.

"In Trinidad, they sell the majority of their crop for export just like you do but they withhold a part for their own consumption and to sell locally. This is where the process is different for the part of their crop that they keep for their own uses. They clean and remove the outer shell of the cocoa seeds. Then, they roast the seeds for about thirty minutes. Next, they grind it-- sometimes by hand and sometimes in a diesel-powered mill like you use here to grind corn into flour. This releases fats and the seeds turn into a liquid that is called 'cocoa liquor.' The cocoa liquor can then be mixed with sugar and milk or other ingredients. They pour it into a mold and let it stand to make a solid block of chocolate. With a common kitchen grater or even a knife, a person can grate the chocolate right into the cup and pour hot water or milk over it for a delicious morning cup of cocoa.

"Now, I ask you," Kenneth concluded, "why couldn't you produce these blocks of high-quality, good tasting local chocolate and sell it to the street food vendors? I'll bet you could beat the imported chocolate on price and on taste. Don't forget the power of patriotism, too. Why not call it 'AfriChoco' or something similar? Every time a street vendor makes a cup for his customer and every time the customer drinks --and enjoys--his morning cup, they're striking a blow for the country's development, consuming a local product and rejecting an imported one!"

The group became animated and again broke up into several competing conversations but this time they were delighted with Kenneth's proposal.

Kojovi called for order.

"I don't want to dampen anyone's enthusiasm for Kenneth's scheme," he said. "I like it very much myself but it will be hard work and will require us to learn new skills. We'll need to learn not only how to make our 'AfriChoco' blocks but also how to package, market, and distribute them. We'll need to have a good set of accounts and keep them up-to-date and transparent."

Everyone nodded in agreement.

"First, we owe it to ourselves to do some research." he continued. "Some of us need to learn the techniques and make that sure we have it right. We need to do a market survey and a cost-benefit analysis. Many of our compatriots launch themselves into business with great energy and the best of intentions but without first acquiring the knowledge and skills necessary for success. You know what I mean, don't you? Your neighbor buys a diesel corn mill and is making a good little profit. So, everyone emulates him. Finally, there are a cluster of mills in the village. Each is milling some corn but no one is making any money."

Kenneth joined in.

"If you like," he said, "I'll assemble all the technical guides for artisanal chocolate- making and any other materials that you think will be useful. But I heartilyendorse Kojovi's proposal for a market survey and a cost-benefit analysis. Even though you are obviously very enthusiastic about this project, you will thank yourselves for having the patience and the discipline to be properly prepared."

Kojovi shook Kenneth's hand.

"You didn't flatter us," he said, "and flattery would not have helped us at all. Your proposal is the first specific, practical one that anyone has offered to us. This is worth serious consideration and that's what we'll give it. Thank you."

The young planters group proved to be dynamic and very ambitious. During the next three months until harvest, weeding and clearing under the trees was what required the attention of the planters and their share-croppers from the North. This left them time to pursue the AfriChoco idea.

The group's members were a diverse bunch in their skills and academic training. They jumped into the effort and self-divided into task groups along the lines that Kojovi had outlined.

One team focused on acquiring the information on Trinidad's artisanal chocolate production from Kenneth and trying to replicate what was in the documents. They built drying frames. They identified mills that could shell the dried beans and others that could grind them into liquid. They fabricated molds for the chocolate blocks. At each step, they carefully noted the time, skills, and cost required. They were also careful to document the processes involved in each step. Finally, they confronted the important question of hygiene. Everyone was agreed that a batch contaminated by disease, such as salmonella, could simultaneously sicken and even kill their customers and, of course, destroy AfriChoco's reputation among actual and potential consumers.

Another team dealt with the all-important cost-benefit analysis and market survey. For team members who had some economic training, an analysis was pretty straight-forward. A classic cost-benefit analysis, however, relies on a great deal of written information, including public records, most of which would be either non-existent or unavailable to the planters.

"We have to create our own shoe-leather CBA," the team's leader concluded.

"Or rather, our own rubber-sandal CBA," another member chimed in to the delight of the group.

"Quite right, my friend," agreed the team leader with a grin. "We need to go out and interview the planters, and even the planters' sharecroppers, the street vendors, and the housewives in their kitchens. We need to find out what their costs and tastes and preferences are. Also, we need information about the costs and conditions of transport and of those who supply us with the goods and tools that we need. In short, we need to get the information orally that we otherwise might access in written form."

The group put their heads together and came up with a list of questions that interviewers would ask the different targets of their study. The questions would unearth the basic numbers that a CBA required so that they could be consolidated and analyzed. The team recruited other members, trained them to use the questionnaire, and fanned out, beginning with their own district and then to the market towns and district capitals of their region and finally to Lomé.

"We must do what the other teams do," reminded another member. "We need to document not only our results and reports but also our experiences in carrying out our CBA. In the future, if we or others need to replicate our rubber-sandal CBA, it's sure that they won't learn how to do it from a textbook!"

Team Three addressed logistics and management, especially the distribution of AfriChoco bars to customers and collecting and accounting for payment.

Team Four set up the founding documents of the business. Following the law carefully, they established AfriChoco as a cooperative business. Under co-op law, the business was governed democratically--one person, one vote--while profits were shared equitably according to each member's level of participation.

Kojovi held his breath when he saw how much each of the young planters wanted to hold off the market that first season to contribute to the AfriChoco pool.

"What if AfriChoco doesn't work?" he worried. "What if everyone has been encouraging us out of sheer kindness? God knows, in our culture, we don't like to discourage anyone. What if they didn't really like our product and were just being polite and they ended up not buying any of it? What if we have a quality problem, or a logistics breakdown, or theft?"

Kojovi needn't have worried. AfriChoco sold briskly. To bridge the time before the next year's harvest, they had to buy additional cocoa from planters who were not part of their cooperative. As they prepared for the second year harvest, AfriChoco's popularity was spreading among both the roadside sellers and the modest households that they targeted. Rather than fearing that they might devote too much of their harvest for chocolate production, they worried that they might reserve too little of it.

The second year was even more successful than their experimental first year. They got down to business. They acted aggressively and dynamically and the local marketplace rewarded them. AfriChoco was growing in number of co-op members and growing in net income to the participating planters. The planters began to believe that a middle class existence just might be possible from their agriculture and their agribusiness.

When the young AfriChoco planters and their families were invited to a meeting with not only the Préfet but also the Director-General of the Coffee and Cocoa Promotion Agency, they were delighted but they were not really surprised. They arrived in their best attire because they expected to be recognized and complimented for their initiative and their achievements. They were sure that they would be thanked for their contributions to Togo's economic development and independence. True to their expectations, the Director-General began by praising the young people. It quickly became clear, however, that thanks were not the purpose of the assembly.

"I regret to inform you," the Director-General continued, his face transformed from a smile to a frown, "that the government has forbidden the production, distribution, and sale of AfriChoco--effective immediately."

There was silence. The young people looked at each other with open-mouthed astonishment before leaping to their feet and surging toward the speakers with loud cries of protest accompanied by brandished clenched fists. The Préfet had been wise to request that the delegation be accompanied not by local *gardiens de préfecture* nor by police but by a small detachment of paramilitary *gendarmes*. The *gendarmes* were well-trained in the art of controlling the population and they had only to advance toward the crowd with nightsticks in hand and pistols still in their holsters to accomplish their mission. The young men and women quickly retreated to their seats or to the back door but continued their verbal protest.

"We are all supporters of the President and the Party," the AfriChoco president addressed the speakers and his friends became quiet. "We have returned to the soil, even after gaining our education, just as the General asked us to do for the good of our country. And now you crush us--why?"

"AfriChoco is a manufactured food item," the Director-General replied. "The artisanal production of AfriChoco and its hand-packaging and distribution do not meet production standards according to manufacturing law and do not meet health standards according to the Public Health Protection Service. Therefore, it is with the public interest in mind that you must cease to fabricate AfriChoco."

This "public interest" was, of course, a flimsy and transparent excuse that was used by the government to cover the real motive behind its action. The importation of items like instant coffee and powdered cocoa was being affected negatively--not much at this stage, but potentially more--by the increasing popularity of AfriChoco. It was the wealthy market women called *Nana Benz* and the Lebanese merchants who were the importers of instant coffee and powdered cocoa whose business was threatened by the increasing market share taken by AfriChoco. They intervened directly with the decision makers in the government who saw that their own interests were at stake. Anything that negatively affected their benefactors in the business community affected them as well.

The following day, the President of AfriChoco went to see the local Préfet at his office and protested the actions. The Préfet, who was from the region, was willing to make a few comments off the record.

"You have to understand," the Préfet said, "that exporting coffee and cocoa brings the government revenues. Replacing the imports by AfriChoco does not bring us any foreign exchange or any replacement of the money that the government would get from exporting coffee and cocoa. Its fabrication and sale is so decentralized, it would be very difficult to tax. To make up the revenue lost from export would be a great inconvenience. I do not need to tell you that there are entrenched business interests that are threatened by AfriChoco. There is nothing that I can do. You can make your AfriChoco and enjoy it among yourselves but you cannot package it, distribute it, or sell it. That is final."

When the AfriChoco cooperative reconvened, the president had invited a group of young women to join them. Before he introduced them, however, he recounted his meeting with the Préfet. When he had finished, one of the young planters leaped to his feet.

"We could export, too," he exclaimed. "If we improve production and we add value by making AfriChoco, we could export it to neighboring countries. In other words, we could replace imports as well as exporting. The country could earn even more foreign exchange and use less of its own foreign currency stocks in order to buy imported cocoa. Don't they understand?"

His intervention went without response.

"Our guests come from down in the foothills of our mountains," said the president. "They have encountered problems similar to ours. Let's listen to what they have to say."

"Our group is composed of young women who pool their resources in a cooperative to improve our lives and that of our families," said Elom, their spokeswoman. "We use palm oil to make indigenous soap with ashes. We improved the process so that it is of higher quality. It forms into a bar instead of the traditional paste and it smells better thanks to some ground flowers that we added. The added value made our local soap more competitive in both quality and price with the imported manufactured soap. Little by little, we have been gaining a share of the market. Our sales are still modest, but we are making a profit and helping our families.

"Recently, however, we had an encounter with the government that was much like yours," she continued. "In our case, the Director General of the State Palm Oil Authority called us together in the company of the Préfet. After complimenting us for our work, he announced that access to palm oil from the Palm Oil Authority facility was cut off. Purchase of palm oil is now restricted to a small amount that could cover only a family's needs for cooking and for small production of soap at home, but not enough to produce for the local marketplace. When we confronted the Préfet, we received the same kinds of the official and unofficial explanations that you received in regard to AfriChoco. The centralization of the palm oil for export was important to gain foreign exchange for the country and revenues for the government.

"It is not just the government," she said, "but also the *Nana Benz* who could be threatened by the popularity of an improved version of the local soap."

Nana Benz was the popular name for Lomé's powerful women merchants who circulated in chauffeur-driven Mercedes vehicles. They were largely composed of Anlo-Éwé transplants from nearby Kéta in Ghana and Minas from the Togo coast. They dominated the cloth importing and re-selling business and gained an international reputation for their business acumen, their cut-throat tactics, and their political influence. Many were literate in Éwé but not in French and could do a million dollars turnover in a year while keeping all "the books" in their heads! They flew to visit manufacturers of the colorful so-called "Dutch wax" cloth to consult with them on new patterns and negotiate contracts.

"The *Nana Benz* are not only in the cloth business; they also control the importation of soaps from the European-owned factories in Ivory Coast and in Nigeria, as well as in Europe. To replace imports of soap with a local product over which they had no control directly threatened their bottom line. You already know that there is no single group of people who have more influence with the government than the *Nana Benz*. We will no longer be given unlimited access to buying palm oil from the palm oil authority's plantations and that is final. We do not have enough palm trees on our own farms to do anything more than fulfill to our families' needs. Developing a palm oil plantation of our own is possible but it would take years before the production was large enough for us to begin again."

When the soap makers had finished speaking, the planters group's anger was boiling over.

"We have got to do something," Kojovi said as he tried to rally his colleagues. "This is unacceptable. This is our country. We have the right to make a living and to try to improve our lives just like anyone else."

One of the other young women joined in.

"There is nothing we can do about these situations," she said. "As for the soap, we will abandon our efforts. We are going to have to find something else that we can do to make money."

"Well, I know one thing we can do," the Kojovi announced. "We can show them that this is no small matter to us. We can strike. We can hold our products off the market. If they will not let us make AfriChoco, then we will hold our cocoa off the market until they relent and allow us to do what we want. If they do not have any cocoa, then they will have even less foreign exchange and less money than they would if they allowed us to produce AfriChoco!"

"You must be careful, my friend," said one of the young planters as he slowly stood up. "You are putting your foot into dangerous territory by challenging the government. The dockers at the Port of Lomé went on strike after a number of their members were hurt badly. They were paid a ridiculously low wage to do very dangerous work. The General ordered the dockers union members to the Hall of the People--all three or four thousand of them--for a meeting at four o'clock in the morning. He told them that they were lucky to have jobs in a country where jobs are very scarce and condemned them for their irresponsible actions and lack of patriotism. He made a very weak commitment to try to improve the safety of their working conditions. He reminded them that he called them to the meeting at an early hour because this gave them plenty of time to get to work at the port at the usual hour of six o'clock. They returned to work and that was the end of it.

"No group has ever dared confront the government since that time. The union leaders lost their positions. The unions are nothing but branches of the of the Party. They carry the party line down from on high but do not represent their members. So, it is not wise for us to think about confronting the government. In fact, it is dangerous. We have to put our heads together and find something else to do that will not lead us into conflict with the government.

"Besides," he concluded, "since we grow export crops and buy food, how will we eat if we are not selling our crops?"

"What if we can find a way to produce more local food, something that does not compete with the *Nana Benz*," someone else wondered aloud. "What if..."

The group became silent. A pall had fallen over them. They looked beaten and dispirited. They were hurt that their own government would blindside them.

"We have got to wait until Kenneth comes back on his next trip," said Kojovi. "He got us into this mess. It is time for him to tell us what we can do, to tell us what our next move should be, to tell us how we can make money from our agriculture and still not tangle with the government."

The group nodded in assent and broke up.

There would not be another opportunity to consult with Kenneth. A United Nations expert cannot do anything that is counter to the wishes of the host country's government. After all, who are the members of the United Nations? The governments! In advising the young planters of AfriChoco in a way that led them to act contrary to the government's interests, Kenneth had crossed the line. He was declared *persona non grata* by the government to the great amusement of his colleagues in the expatriate assistance community.

"It's a badge of honor to be *PNG*'d by one of these petty dictators," they told him. "Sooner or later, it happens to us all, formally or informally."

AfriChoco was a stimulating experiment for him. Kenneth already knew about the role that the *Nana Benz* and the Lebanese played in the economy. FAO and other agencies had studied their economic and political influence extensively. Their reports abounded and were updated regularly. Therefore, he wasn't surprised when the government strangled AfriChoco and the soap-making scheme. It was fascinating, worthy perhaps of an article in an academic journal. The risks to him in the experiment were negligible. As for the risks to his young followers, he never stopped to calculate them. He had no regrets.

Kenneth was no longer an expert for the Food and Agriculture Organization. He had moved on. Just as he planned except a few years earlier, Kenneth went to work for one of the large cocoa corporations at a salary that was even higher and with benefits even more ample than the ones that he received at the FAO.

On the rare occasions when he did visit Togo after his *PNG*-status was lifted, he did not come back to the AfriChoco region. He sent his young protégés greetings through an intermediary. He preferred to visit the region around Yégué on the North side of the Plateau Region. The government had built a new paved road to Yégué that stopped at the Ghana border, all the better to bring out not only Togolese coffee and cocoa but also that which was smuggled into the country. In Ghana, many planters and buyers preferred to be paid in hard currency rather than in the Ghanaian currency, the cedi.

There is a rumor that AfriChoco is still being produced. They say that the street sellers grate it into the familiar green powdered cocoa tins every night before setting up their stands the next morning. There is also a rumor that one of the foreign chocolate companies is going to change the colors of its tins and rename their product ... AfriChoco!

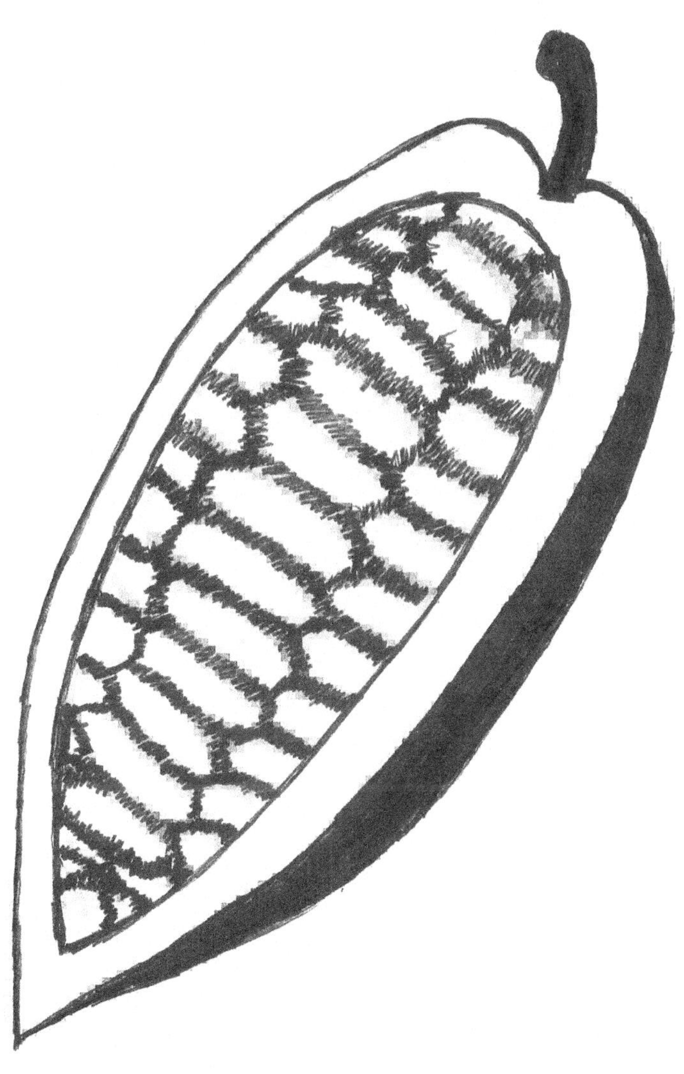

ACKNOWLEDGMENTS

This collection of short fiction was more than a quarter century in the making--longer if I count the fact that I wrote several of the stories "in my head" years before putting them to paper. I am very grateful to the friends and colleagues who have encouraged me to write and to those who contributed their time and expertise to reading and offering constructive criticism of my drafts. A very special thanks goes to Meredith Pike-Baky whose critiques and suggestions have been of inestimable value and helped me to move these stories along to completion and publication.

My friend Anne Todd responded to my request for suggestions for the book's cover by selecting Sheena O'Brien's beautiful photograph of a Togolese beach scene with the Lomé skyline in the distance and by designing the layout. My son Diego Morris added the cover lettering. My thanks to all three of them.

The back cover photograph depicting a two-story Tamberma house near Tchitchirra in Doufelgou Préfecture, Togo, was taken by me in 1969.

The Water Witch was read on the BBC World Service Radio Program, *Short Story*, on March 11, 12, and 14, 1984. It was also published in the Autumn 1985 edition of **SELAMTA**, the in-flight magazine of Ethiopian Airlines. When BBC broadcast and **SELAMTA** published my first story, I was proud of the recognition of my writing and was encouraged to continue to write.

The short story, **AfriChoco**, first saw the light of day in 1986, but not as a short story. My original goal was to write a teleplay that would be suitable for Togolese television. There were frequent locally-produced plays on Togolese television that were very enjoyable. One of the enduring characters in the Togolese televised plays was a fellow known around town by the name of the character he portrayed in several of the television productions--"Politicos." I never knew his real name and neither did most of his fans. Originally, the name of the teleplay that became a short story was **ChocoTogo**.

In 2016, I was delighted to learn that some young Togolese entrepreneurs had created a fair-trade cooperative company called **ChocoTogo.** It transforms locally-produced cocoa into products for the local market and for export such as cocoa paste and dark chocolate with different flavors derived from other organic products like peanuts, ginger, coconut, and lemon. I am very pleased that someone in Togo has finally taken the initiative to transform and commercialize Togolese cocoa. In order to avoid any confusion, I changed the name of my short story from **ChocoTogo** to **AfriChoco.** I wish **ChocoTogo** the best of luck.

FRIENDS OF TOGO / *LES AMIS DU TOGO*

Friends of Togo (FoT) is a non-profit educational and service organization created in 1981 by Returned Peace Corps Volunteers and staff who served in Togo, West Africa. Membership is not restricted to Togo RPCVs and staff. They are joined by family members and friends, by diplomats, aid workers, businesspeople, and missionaries who have served in Togo, by Togolese nationals living outside of their country, and by others who are interested in Togo.

FoT members seek to fulfill Peace Corps' Third Goal mission of bringing their experience back home by maintaining contact with Togo and its people, by sharing experiences with their fellow Americans, and by continuing to assist Togo's development. FoT raises funds for micro-projects and for modest contributions to school expenses in Togo; sponsors group flights to Togo; organizes picnics and other social events; and participates in educating the public about Togo, Africa, and development.

To join Friends of Togo, send $25 US annual dues ($35US international) & any contributions for micro-projects and modest student assistance to: **FRIENDS OF TOGO, INC., P.O. BOX 533, PORTAGE, WI 53901 USA**

Visit the **FRIENDS OF TOGO on the Web** at:
https://www.peacecorpsconnect.org/companies/friends-of-togo

Or follow them on Facebook at "Friends of Togo/Amis du Togo".

You can keep in contact with friends and colleagues on our **Friends of Togo** discussion group on Google Groups.

To join send a message to friends-of-togo@googlegroups.com

Follow **Friends of Togo** and news about Togo on **Twitter** at **TogoTweet:** twitter.com/TogoTweet

ABOUT THE AUTHOR

Kelly J. Morris is a writer, editor, translator, and independent consultant. For more than thirty years he worked in international development, principally with the Peace Corps (19 years) and the World Council of Credit Unions - WOCCU (10 years). He lived in Africa for fourteen years and, when based in the US, traveled frequently to Africa. He is the author of another short story collection, **Fire in the Tree: The Inspector Toh-jay Stories,** and of **Playing the Notes That Aren't There: Africa Since 1969, Essays, Articles, and Reminiscences**. His next books, **African Democracy: A Primer for Development Workers** and **Let the Big Cat Jump**, a collection of short stories set in his home state of West Virginia, will appear in 2021. He has contributed chapters to several books: **Shelter** (Shelter Publications); **Credit Unions and the Poverty Challenge** (ILO); and **One Hand Does Not Catch a Buffalo: 50 Years of Amazing Peace Corps Stories, Volume One: Africa.** His writing has been published in **American Diplomacy.** His short story, **The Water Witch**, was broadcast on the BBC World Service radio program, **Short Story,** and published in **SELAMTA**, the in-flight magazine of Ethiopian Airlines..

In the early years of his career, Mr. Morris supported rural community development activities in community self-help construction, animal traction extension, cooperatives, and school agricultural education. By the early 1980s, his technical focus broadened to include credit unions, co-operatives, microfinance, and microenterprise.. After serving as resident technical advisor to the Togo Credit Union Federation, he moved to WOCCU's Home Office where he developed and managed a multi-million dollar portfolio of

USAID-funded credit union development projects. In the mid-1990s, he broadened his technical focus once again to add information and communications technologies for development (ICT4D). He was Peace Corps Headquarters' principal "ICTs Evangelist" for several years, eventually becoming its first official ICT Program Specialist. He coordinated the agency's ICT Initiative and originated and managed the ICT Training-of-Trainers activity.

In recent years, Mr. Morris has expanded his geographic focus to include the Arab world and the larger Muslim world, including North Africa, the Middle East, and Central and South Asia. He is particularly interested in promoting savings and credit cooperatives (i.e. credit unions) that embrace the principles and practices of Islamic Finance. He has advised several Muslim groups in the United States on the creation of Islamic credit unions.

Mr. Morris is a graduate of Duke University with a Bachelor of Arts (AB) degree in History (European, African, and Chinese). He is a Certified Credit Union Executive (CCUE). He speaks French, has a working knowledge of two West African languages--Mina and Nawdm--and has studied Brazilian Portuguese.

In 1981, Mr. Morris founded and was first president of the Friends of Togo/Les Amis du Togo (FoT). FoT stimulated the creation of more than 50 country-of-service groups by Returned Peace Corps Volunteers and staff using the *Friends of ___* model. In 1997, he created and was List Owner of Togo-L, the FoT mailing list ("listserv"), that has more than 800 subscribers.

SUGGESTIONS FOR FURTHER READING

Until the last few years, there were very few books in English about the Bight of Benin countries, especially the Francophone countries of Togo and Bénin, For those readers who would like to learn more about these countries and their peoples, I recommend the following books:

1. My old friend Mark Wentling is the author of a trilogy: ***Africa's Embrace, Africa's Release***, and ***Africa's Heart***. Mark became a Peace Corps Volunteer in Togo in 1970 and there began more than 40 years in Africa with Peace Corps, USAID, and PVOs. Memoirs in the form of novels, they are the fascinating tale of a young American man who leaves Kansas to go to Africa to help the poor. He adjusts to life in an African village and acquires the African name, Bobovovi, but he finds his mission fraught with many

unforeseen and unusual challenges.

The books contain a delightful mixture of magical realism and the practical challenges of living and working in Africa in the early 1970s. They introduce a cast of unforgettable characters and take the reader on a rollicking African adventure.

2. In ***To Benin and Back: Short Stories, Essays, and Reflections About Life in Benin as a Peace Corps Volunteer and the Subsequent Readjustment Process***, Bénin RPCV Chris Starace gleaned the most interesting stories, anecdotes, cultural observations, essays and reflections about his experiences in Benin as well about his acute reverse culture shock when he returned to the U.S.

For more information about the book go to tobeninandback.com. It is also available in e-book formats such as Kindle on Amazon.com and Nook on BarnesandNoble.com.

3. Lawrance, Benjamin N., ***Locality, Mobility, and "Nation": Periurban Colonialism in Togo's Eweland 1900-1960***, (Rochester, NY: University of Rochester Press), 2007.

Since Lawrance's book is the only history in English of Southern Togo during the colonial period, we are extremely fortunate that it is such a good one. He fills in gaps in information about this critical period in Togo's history and gives it its most thorough and objective treatment. His treatment of the Ewe Reunification movement is most insightful and his application of the peri-urban organization model to Éwéland is a very helpful and accurate depiction of the region.

4. Chernoff, John M., ***Hustling is Not Stealing: Stories of an African Bar Girl***, (Chicago: University of Chicago Press), 2003, and Chernoff, John M., ***Exchange is Not Robbery: More Stories of an African Bar Girl***, Chicago: University of Chicago Press), 2005.

I bought Chernoff's two books several years ago. After quickly skimming the contents, however, I put them on a shelf and did not take them down again until after I had completed writing my first two books. The reason: Chernoff was in Ghana during much of the same time that I was in Togo and visited Ghana regularly in the 1970s. I wanted to avoid being influenced by his writing. When I finally did read his books, the parallels between his experiences and mine were evident, sometimes eerily so (e.g. he had a friend whose nickname was Santana as did the main character of my story, *The Water Witch*--both nicknamed after Santana's performance at the *Soul to Soul* concert in Accra in 1971). After a lengthy introduction by Chernoff, most of the two books is devoted to the stories told by a bar-girl named Hawa who was born in Ghana of Burkinabè parents. Chernoff collected her stories over a period of years as she moved between Ghana, Togo, and Burkina Faso. She proved to be a "virtuoso storyteller" with a "perceptive intellect" and "observational skills"--a "seeker as well as a storyteller." In Hawa, Chernoff gives us access to what is so often missing from books about Africa: the authentic voices of ordinary African people in their own words, especially girls and women, who struggle with poverty while maintaining their dignity. Her portrayal of the lives of average (i.e. mostly poor) people rings absolutely true. We may not have known the same people, but her descriptions and analysis fit closely the people that I did know. If you are interested in "girls education and empowerment" in Africa, I would suggest that you start with Chernoff's books.

5. Piot, Charles, ***Remotely Global: Village Modernity in West Africa***, (Chicago: University of Chicago Press), 1999. In this book, Charles Piot demolishes one of the most pernicious myths about Africa and Africans. Africa, we have been told, is timeless and unchanging and Africans live much as their ancestors did for centuries or even millennia, untouched by

modernity. Piot's account of his life among the Kabyè people in and around Farrendé in Northern Togo demonstrates clearly that even remote communities were active participants in the world around them. They adapted to changing circumstances while still maintaining their own culture, adopting from others new practices that they found useful without capitulating to their bearers.

Piot also explodes the Togolese myth that the Kabyè people are an inherently violent people with a militaristic culture. The Kabyè are an extremely hard-working people who made productive the rocky slopes and nearby lands where they had fled from slave-raiders. Many, but not all, Kabyè communities participate in the annual *évala* wrestling competitions that mark the passage of young men from adolescence to young adulthood. The colonialists targeted the Kabyè and their neighbors for military service in defense of the *métropole* and for slave labor and fabricated myths to justify their practices. To the chagrin of many Kabyè elders, the late Gen. Gnassingbé Éyadéma exploited *évala* to help recruit an army that was loyal to him and justified the practice by claiming that the Kabyè are more suited for military service by virtue of their culture. Piot is witness to the fact that they are a friendly, non-aggressive, and non-violent people.

*See also **Nostalgia for the Future: West Africa after the Cold War,*** (Chicago: University of Chicago Press), 2010 and ***The Fixer: Visa Lottery Chronicles (Theory in Forms)***(Duke University Press Books), 2019.

6. Morrow, Curtis J. "Kojo," ***Return of the African-American***, (Huntington, NY: Kroshka Books), 2000. When Ghana became independent in 1957, President Kwame Nkrumah invited Africans of the Diaspora to "come home" and put their skills and energy to the service of building the new nation. One of those who responded was Curtis Morrow, a combat veteran of America's forgotten war in Korea, who was wounded twice and

awarded the Bronze Star, the Combat Infantry Badge, and four Battle Stars. He was an artist who increasingly chafed under the oppressive racial discrimination of the U.S. in the 1950s and 1960s. Finally, in 1965, he scraped together enough money from his job as a night porter at a post office to buy a round-trip plane ticket to Accra. He intended to "test the waters" and return after a few weeks if what he found was not to his liking. He stayed for eleven years. His book is the moving story of his time living in Ghana, Togo, and Côte d'Ivoire and his lifelong connection to Africa.

7. Charlés, Laurie L., ***Intimate Colonialism: Head, Heart, and Body in West African Development Work***, (Walnut Creek, CA: Left Coast Press), 2007. Laurie Charlés, a Ph.D. in family therapy and an ethnographic researcher, describes her Volunteer service in Togo in the Girls Education and Empowerment Program from 1999 to 2001. She addresses not only the sexual oppression of girls in Togo but also, in what is called "an autoethnographic exploration of the self," she frankly portrays the exploration of her own sexuality while integrating into Togolese society.

8. Chatwin, Bruce. ***The Viceroy of Ouidah***. (New York: Penguin Books), 1988. In this novel by the late travel writer and novelist, Bruce Chatwin, he tells the story of Francisco Manoel de Silva, a Brazilian adventurer who set himself up in Ouidah, Dahomey (now Bénin) where he became enormously wealthy in the slave trade. The novel is based on the real life of Francisco Felix de Sousa, a Brazilian slave trader of Portuguese origin in what was then called *The Slave Coast*, present-day Togo and Bénin. de Sousa earned the confidence of King Ghezo of Dahomey who made him Viceroy of the slave port of Ouidah. He dominated the slave trade in the area in the late 1700s though the mid-1800s, continuing long after the slave trade had been made illegal by most countries.

9. Kourouma, Ahmadou, ***Waiting for the Wild Beasts to Vote***,

(Vintage), 2004. Kourouma was a prolific and renowned novelist from Côte d'Ivoire who went into extended exile from his home country after running afoul of President Félix Houphouet-Boigny. He spent a decade of his exile in Lomé, Togo, where he worked by day in the re-insurance business and rose early each morning to write before work. In this translation of Kourouma's award-winning novel, *En attendant le vote des bêtes sauvages*, the protagonist is based on the thirty-eight year dictator of Togo, Gen. Gnassingbè Éyadéma, who died in 2005.

10. Olinto, Antonio, *The Water House*, (Carroll & Graf), 1986. This book is a translation from Brazilian Portuguese of Olinto's historical novel, *A Casa da Água.* It portrays the return of a family of former slaves from Brazil to West Africa in the nineteenth century. Many of the "returnee" families--often of mixed African, Portuguese, and Amerindian parentage-- became prominent and wealthy along the coast of the Bight of Benin where they were successful merchants, including participating in both the transatlantic and internal slave trade. They married into the local elite and eventually lost all direct contact with Brazil but continued to identify themselves as Brazilians until after the African countries' independence. In this historical novel, the DaRocha family returns to Africa and settles in Lagos, Nigeria. It is there that they prosper, based originally on their business, the Water House, one of the few sources of fresh water in the area. Alinto uses this novel to tell the story of the family of Togo's first President and first dictator, Sylvanus Olympio, who was assassinated in a military coup in 1963.

11. Kpomassie, Tété-Michel, *An African in Greenland*, (New York: Harcourt Brace Jovanovich), 1983. From *National Geographic* to ethnographic studies, we are accustomed to Europeans and North Americans going off to study other peoples, especially in Africa. Kpomassie, who was

born in Togo, reversed the tables. He became obsessed with Greenland and its people after reading a children's book about it in his home town in Togo. He set off for Greenland via France and after 10 years persistence, arrived in Greenland where he lived for several years. He describes the people with whom he lived with an outsider's perspective and with compassion and has maintained a life-long relationship with the people of Greenland that he came to know.

12. Barlow, Aaron, Ed., ***One Hand Does Not Catch a Buffalo: 50 Years of Amazing Peace Corps Stories, Volume One: Africa***, (Palo Alto: Travelers Tales), 2011. This collection of Returned Peace Corps Volunteer tales includes three from Togo (including my story, ***Yaka***), two from Ghana, two from Bénin, one from Nigeria, and several from neighboring West African countries. You will also enjoy Barlow's novel, ***Hard As Kerosene***, that is available as a Kindle ebook.

Books in English about Nigeria and Ghana by Nigerian and Ghanaian authors are more numerous and available.

13. **Nigeria** -- I particularly liked the books of Nigerian writers Chinua Achebe (***Things Fall Apart, No Longer at Ease, A Man of the People, The Arrow of God,*** and ***Anthills of the Savannah***); Wole Soyinka, playwright and poet, winner of the ***Nobel Prize for Literature*** (I liked the memoir of his youth, ***Aké: The Years of Childhood);*** and Amos Tutuola, who wrote ***The Palm-Wine Drinkard*** and ***My Life in the Bush of Ghosts.*** A more recent novel is ***Sozaboy--A Novel in Rotten English***, by the late Ken Saro-Wiwa, a campaigner on behalf of the people of the oil-rich Niger Delta, who was executed by the Nigerian Government. I also enjoyed ***My Mercedes is Bigger Than Yours*** by the late Nkem Nwankwo.

I recommend two biographies by non-Nigerians of famous Nigerians:

Carlos Moore's biography of my favorite musician, Fela Anikulapo-Kuti, entitled *Fela, Fela--This Bitch of a Life;* and Frederick Forsyth's biography of Biafran secessionist leader Chukwuemeka Odumegwu-Ojukwu, entitled *Emeka*.

14. **Ghana** – I enjoyed the writing of novelist Ayi Kwei Armah (*The Beautyful Ones Are Not Yet Born*) and of poet Kofi Awoonor (who was killed in the September 2013 terrorist attack at Westgate shopping mall in Nairobi, Kenya). The writings of Ghana's first President and apostle of African Unity, Kwame Nkrumah, are well worth the read, especially *Ghana: The Autobiography of Kwame Nkrumah, Africa Must Unite, Neo-Colonialism: the Last Stage of Imperialism,* and *African Socialism Revisited*.

Other Books

by

Kelly J. Morris

at

Lulu.com

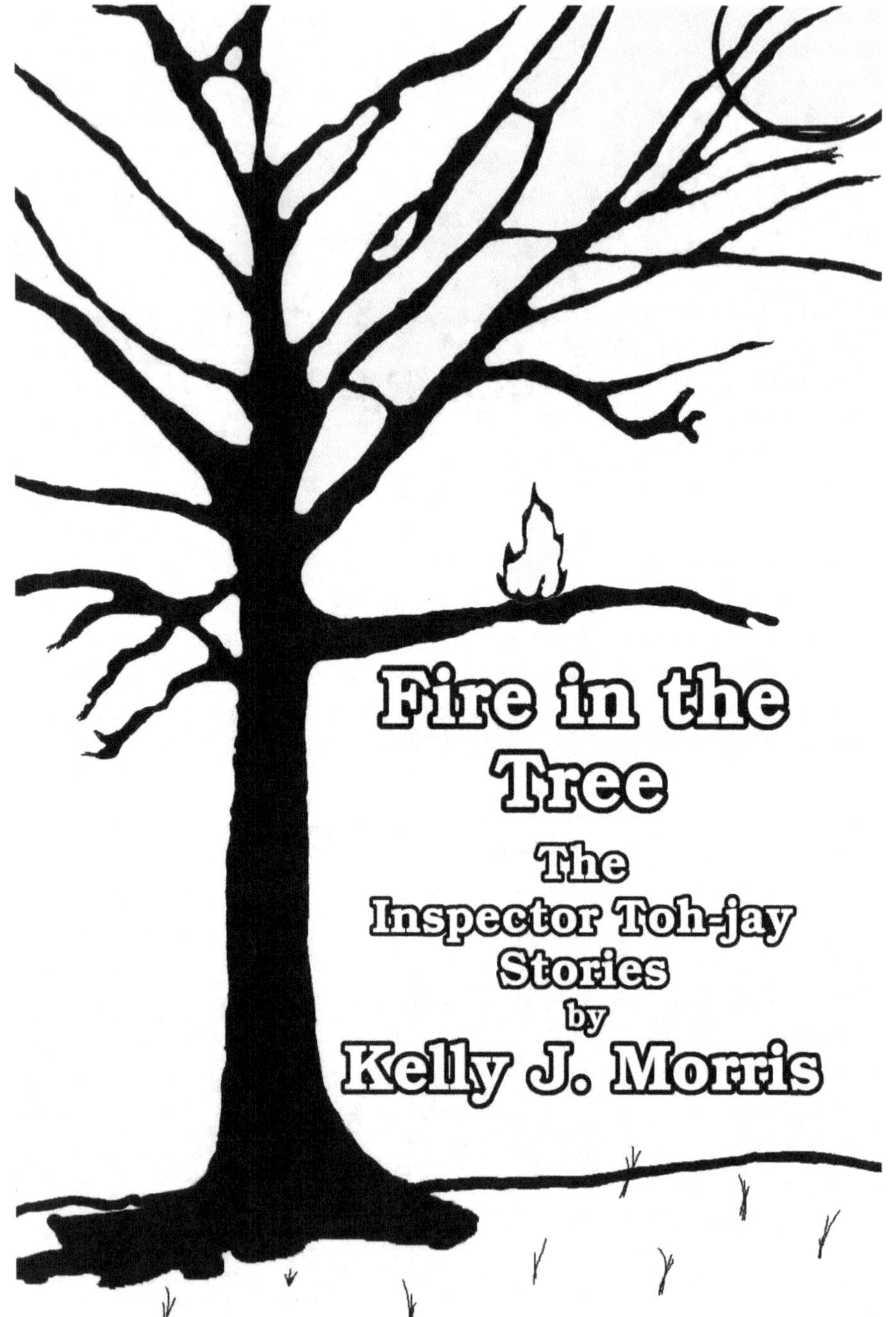
Fire in the
Tree
The
Inspector Toh-jay
Stories
by
Kelly J. Morris

ESSAYS, ARTICLES, AND REMINISCENCES OF AFRICA SINCE 1968

BY

KELLY J. MORRIS

www.ingramcontent.com/pod-product-compliance
Lightning Source LLC
Chambersburg PA
CBHW061759250726
48657CB00001B/195